Contents

KV-639-001

1   Introduction

THIS essay is an immodest attempt to survey the recent literature on urbanization processes in the Third World. Spanning roughly the last ten years, our review covers but a tiny fragment of that vast transformation of cultural landscapes which, according to Kingsley Davis (1972, 48–53), started its course around 1800 and is projected to terminate within another century or so when nearly all of the world's population will be living in cities. We are thus about to raise the curtain on the third act of a drama of truly global dimensions in which we, the spectators, are part of the action itself.

The meaning we assign to urbanization is broad, and our search of the literature has been extensive (Wulff, 1973a). On the one hand, urbanization commonly refers to the concentration of formerly dispersed populations that are primarily engaged in farming in a small number of settlements whose principal economic activities are in the services, trades, and manufactures. A second meaning refers to urban modes of production, living, and thinking originating in these centres and spreading from these to outlying towns and rural populations (Friedmann, 1966a).[1] In either case, and as these processes continue, the social meanings of the landscape are profoundly altered. Studies of urbanization are intent on describing these changes, interpreting their significance, and understanding the social processes which brought them about. They are also concerned with their pathology—the famine, overpopulation, immiseration, dependency, unemployment, and poverty that accompany the spatial transformation— and with the policies that are addressed to these conditions.

Our assessment of the main contributions to the literature—largely but not exclusively restricted to publications in English—is divided into four principal parts:

1   historical studies
2   macro-studies of urbanization processes and patterns
3   micro-studies of urban life
4   policy and planning studies.

Our critique of past research points to a need for a basic reorientation in concept and method. In a concluding part, therefore, we argue that

[1] The implicit assumption in this formulation is that 'innovations' proceed chiefly from urban to rural areas—'down the urban hierarchy and out from core to periphery', as Brian Berry has suggested (Berry and Neils, 1969, 295). This assumption may be wrong or at least one-sided. Under certain assumptions, innovations may also flow in the other direction, 'up from the countryside, and from periphery to core', as the recent experience of China would seem to indicate (Salter, 1974).

The urban transition
Comparative studies of newly industrializing societies

by John Friedmann and
Robert Wulff

Edward

© Edward Arnold (Publishers) Ltd 1975

First published 1976 by
Edward Arnold (Publishers) Ltd
25 Hill Street, London W1X 8LL

ISBN 0 7131 5880 8

Printed in Great Britain by
Butler & Tanner Ltd, Frome and London

studies of urbanization must increasingly support a praxis of social reconstruction and propose a decision-framework as the appropriate theoretical focus.

Historical studies are antithetical to the practice of contemporary social science with its self-confident commitment to the present. Yet many of the culture areas we shall examine once supported flourishing civilizations that ultimately perished, and it is a view of the transitoriness of cities and the life they sustained that provides us with a perspective on the period of historical change through which we ourselves are passing.

Macro-studies of urbanization are characterized by their approach to the subject via the concept of a spatial system that consists of both a 'core' and a 'periphery' (Friedmann, 1973b, chapter 3). Although the systems studied are almost always national, attention has recently shifted to the question of foreign domination and its influence on national spatial patterns and their evolution.

Micro-studies—our third category—have their focus chiefly on facets of life in individual cities: urban morphology, social organization, and mobility; the urban economy, and urban politics and social control. These not unrelated phenomena are taken here under the microscope and studied in considerable detail. Unfortunately no concepts have yet been found to link, within a single and coherent framework, observations at the micro- with those at macro-levels of urbanization. The only theory which claims to have done so is philosophical Marxism (Lefèbvre, 1972). Its holistic method—corresponding to a motivation drawn from revolutionary practice—is particularly well suited for a critical understanding of historical processes; it has yet to prove itself, however, as a method for application to specific policy designs.

A survey of *policy and planning studies* concludes the evaluative part of our review. More explicitly rooted in normative than in empirical considerations, policy 'science' has seized upon the social ills that have acquired salience among policy makers in the newly industrializing countries: the unequal spatial distribution of economic growth and welfare, 'excessive' city populations, and slums and squatter settlements. This set of problems suggests that planners have not yet moved from a pre-occupation with social pathology to social reconstruction. But to accomplish this may well exceed the scope of purely analytical approaches.

Most of the world will be completely urbanized within another hundred years. If unheard-of dimensions of human suffering are not to undermine the very foundations of the policies that are intended to contain and ultimately to eradicate this suffering, we shall have to find entirely new ways for organizing social life. It is in praxis—in appropriate theory wedded to action—that a solution must be found. In the final portion of this essay, we shall therefore turn our attention towards a possible approach to social reconstruction through a decision-framework for innovative planning.

II The city in history

A title such as *The city in history* (Mumford, 1961) begs the intriguing question: what is a city? Within their own culture, Westerners would seem to have little difficulty in replying: Paris, London, and New York are obviously cities. But what about Los Angeles? There are those who would argue that Los Angeles, though clearly urban, no longer is a city but has become an *urban field* (Friedmann and Miller, 1965). Similar problems of conceptualization arise when we descend the urban hierarchy. Wherein, for example, lies the distinction between town and village, especially when a majority of the employment in towns of even ten and twenty thousand souls is found in farming (Bataillon, 1973, 202–3)?

Archaeologists have discovered the question of definition to be equally troublesome. The further back in time they search for traces of urbanism and the origin of cities, the more difficult they find it to establish clear-cut rules by which true city-ness may be distinguished. Was ancient Jericho a city? Or Ankor Wat? And were the remnants of its drainage system a sufficient guarantee that Mohenjo Daro truly was a city? And if so, in what sense? Max Weber (1958) argued, on rather narrow grounds, that the city was exclusively an occidental form; he denied city-ness to other cultures. Although a more ecumenical view was propounded by Gordon Childe (1950), the real difficulty lay elsewhere. For the city is a social microcosm and consequently a multi-dimensional phenomenon displaying a variety of physical, spatial, cultural, institutional, economic, demographic, and social characteristics. Like the blind men examining the elephant, different urban historians would seize upon a single feature of urbanity and proclaim it as the true and only one.

It would seem that there is no easy way out of this impasse. Definitions are useful only in a context, and one or the other definition may be serviceable for the limited purposes at hand. Still, a few notions which have recently gained currency point in a possibly fruitful direction for a wide variety of comparative analysis. As a *social system*, the city suggests intensive interaction and interdependency among its residents and institutions. As a *spatial system*, it suggests that these patterns of interaction are spatially bounded. As a *subsystem of society*, it suggests that the city is part of an encompassing social whole. As a *space-organizing* subsystem it suggests that it also functions as a central place (within a hierarchy of central places) to organize surrounding and sometimes distant territories into economic, social, and cultural spaces (Friedmann, 1961; Wheatley, 1971, 388). Finally, as a *redistributive centre* (Wheatley, 1971, 264–5; Harvey, 1973, 238–40), it suggests the city's control over dependent areas and spatially dispersed populations for the purpose of appropriating (and sometimes redistributing) a surplus from production that will allow the city's population, but especially its rulers, to enrich themselves and further to expand their territorial power. These dependent areas, together with their dominant and hierarchically ordered centres of control, form the basic units of spatial analysis.

This essentially geographic formulation for the comparative and historical study of cities is beginning to be widely used (Johnson, 1972). Cities are no longer seen as independent entities, but as space-organizing systems, and the presumed self-sufficiency of early cities in Mesopotamia (Adams and Nissen, 1972) and Yucatan (Marcus 1973; Green, 1973) has had to yield in the face of mounting evidence that service functions, such as markets and transport, may override soil, water, and defence as basic considerations in the location of urban settlements.

A no less vexing question has been the origin of cities (Kraeling and Adams, 1960; Mumford, 1961; Braidwood and Willey, 1962; Adams, R. McC., 1968; Ucko, Tringham, and Dimbleby, 1972). It may well be, of course, that like the previous one, this question also has no answer. For compact cities are not just suddenly invented like New Towns but represent the culmination of a long period of evolutionary change in the spatial organization of society. To call this 'revolution', as Gordon Childe has done (1950; 1951, chapter 7), is simply verbal sorcery.

The fact is that urban civilizations have emerged in widely separated areas, and distinctive evolutionary sequences of settlement have been identified in each. There is by no means full agreement, however, on the extent to which these represented autochthonous developments, uncorrupted by significant contact with other cultures. And there is the further and related problem (crucial to the question of a presumptive continuity) whether in each area of 'primary' urbanization compact cities emerged as yet another step in the evolution of such proto-urban forms as ceremonial centres, or whether they leaped into being without the benefit of intermediate stages.[2]

[2] Paul Wheatley (1971, 9) suggests seven areas of 'primary' urbanization (i.e., of independent 'invention'): Mesopotamia, the Indus Valley, the Nile Valley, the North China Plain, Mesoamerica, the central Andes, and southwest Nigeria. All other urban civilizations, as in Crete, Southeast Asia, and Etruria, were, according to Wheatley, 'secondary' or derived. But as he is very much aware, given the present state of our knowledge, such a labelling may well be premature.

The *scale* of social organization may provide a possible clue to the nature of the sequence itself. Successive innovations in agricultural production and in the ability to mobilize a surplus above rural subsistence were necessary prerequisites for the growth of central settlements, a sizeable proportion of whose population was *not* producing food. Further innovations in the arts of warfare and administration permitted cities to exert a dominant influence over increasingly larger areas, while innovations in trade and manufactures (Jacobs, 1969) enhanced urban pre-eminence and, in time, helped to articulate far-flung and complex spatial systems (Polyani, Arensberg and Pearson, 1957; Mabogunje, 1968). This progressive expansion of urban domains, proceeding outwards from a number of spatially dispersed central points of dominance was limited only by the resistance encountered on the expanding frontier (nomadic barbarians, urban domains expanding from another direction, natural barriers such as deserts and mountains) and by the ability of the central authorities to maintain order in the occupied areas and to supply and maintain the loyalty of their advancing troops (Tekeli, 1973). As the domain expanded, it proved necessary to establish urban outposts as administrative and military centres of control to 'pacify' the native populations and to ensure the orderly collection of a surplus and its transfer to the central rulers, but also as staging areas for further military probes on the frontier.

This rather grim picture of conquest, coercive authority, and exploitation must be softened, however, to the extent that urban rule extended substantial benefits to the populations it controlled and so acquired a *moral authority* as well. Most striking in this connection is Paul Wheatley's (1971, 218) interpretation of the Chou dynasty ceremonial centre as 'the axis of the kingdom, where alone the ruler could seek counsel and intercession from the ancestors who had served the state in the past and now watched over its future, where alone he could preside over the universall harmony that, under the virtuous monarch, manifested itself in the spontaneous cooperation of animate and inanimate nature, and where alone at the pivot of the universe he could ensure the continuance of the cosmic process'.

This was gross mystification, but it also was a shared belief that emphasized, as the basis for community, a perceived relation between the social order and the city. Wherever urban institutions extended their domain, they would attempt to impose a sense of social equilibrium; to provide protection against natural and supernatural disasters; to spread technologies that permitted men to raise themselves above brute poverty; and to foster transcendental beliefs in men's proper relations to the universe.

On a more mundane level than Wheatley's panegyric, Adams's (1972) demonstration of the crucial role of Mesopotamian cities in helping semisedentary populations on the frontier to survive periodic droughts and starvation may serve as yet another instance of the kind of civic order which cities often created. 'Whatever the social cost in exploitation,' he writes (p. 31), 'cities made possible a greater measure of stability, for their dependencies as well as for their own populations, than would have been possible otherwise. That stability alone permitted the cultural and institutional features by which we identify Mesopotamian society as a civilization not only to develop but to acquire the force and continuity of a tradition.'

The study of urban history, however, is not confined to illuminating the difficult problem of urban origins. As the scope of historical inquiry became global, the role of cities in societal change and as crucibles for the moulding of cultural forms became a major focus for research. Early attempts to write global history from the vantage point of the city tended to be more speculative than grounded in careful research; the universal histories of Oswald Spengler (1926–8; original edn. 1918–22), Ralph Turner (1941), Griffith Taylor (1946), and Lewis Mumford (1961) were grand exercises in hermeneutics. But eventually they gave rise to more measured analyses in specific time-space contexts. With their monumental compendium on the area, population, and density of cities on four continents for the past 3,000 years, Chandler and Fox (1974) have provided a quantitative scaffolding for this effort.

Active research is now going forward in a number of geographical areas. Among the outstanding recent contributions we might cite the work of Lapidus (1967), Lampl (1968), Issawi (1969), and Abu-Lughod (1971) on Middle Eastern cities; of Miner (1953), Lloyd, Mabogunje and Awe (1967) and Mabogunje (1968) on urbanization in Central and West Africa; of Morse (1958; 1962; 1971b; 1972) and Harris (1971) on the Latin American city; of Yazaki (1968), Smith, T. C. (1960), and Smith, R. J. (1973) on the social history of cities in Japan; of Spodek (1973) and Shah, A. M. (1973) on nineteenth-century Indian cities; of Chang (1963) and Skinner (1968) on the city in China; and of Karpat (1971) and Tekeli (1973) on urbanization in the Ottoman Empire.

In a rather special category is Robert McC. Adams's *The evolution of urban society* (1966). This was the first serious attempt at a systematic, cross-cultural comparison of social organization in two very different urban domains: Mesopotamia and pre-Hispanic Mexico. The basic thesis of the book, in overt contradiction to the then current ecological models (Wittfogel, 1957, 12), is that 'it seems to have been primarily changes in social institutions that precipitated changes in technology, subsistence, and other aspects of the wider cultural realm, such as religion, rather than vice versa.' This formulation, of course, leaves the fundamental question unanswered of why homologous social forms emerged in areas so

9

widely set apart in space and time that no permanent contact would seem to have been possible. Is it conceivable that Babylon and Tenochtitlan were both perhaps prefigured in the genetic code of their respective founders? If this were so, it would upset some of our most cherished convictions about man's ultimate ability to 'make himself'.

In the context of the present essay, the names above are merely 'calling cards'. It would be quite impossible, in the restricted space we have, to do full justice to the many interpretations and insights of these scholars. All of them, however, provide a healthy antidote to the facile generalizations of those social scientists who are inclined to think that the start of urbanization in Third World countries coincided more or less with the beginning of their own interest in the study of this process. The historians' love of the unique and his insistence on variety, his view of history as cyclical, his acceptance of the possibility of breakdown, stagnation, and decline of whole civilizations, and his search for the 'interior' meaning of events stands in sharp contrast to the social scientists' preoccupation with universal laws, statistical regularities, and equilibrium. Lacking an historical perspective, social scientists are more than prone to sin in the direction of a simple determinism in interpreting their data. By accounting for present patterns and behaviour in terms of intermediate and constraining variables, they think to have demonstrated their inevitability. And by projecting recent trends, they arrive at optimistic/pessimistic versions of the future. The ironic mode of the historian (Muller, 1952) is not congenial to their temper. *Savoir pour prévoir* is still their motto, and they haruspicate in order to predict and to control.

III Macro-studies of urbanization processes and patterns

Urbanization has traditionally been studied by demographers skilled in the measurement of rates of change in urban growth, the components of this growth, and the changing ratios of rural and urban populations. Until quite recently, demographic analysis was almost all there was to the macro-study of urbanization. The classical example is Adna Weber's book on nineteenth-century urbanization in the United States, originally published in 1899 (Weber, A. F., 1965).

Weber's modern counterpart, but working now at an appropriate global scale, is Kingsley Davis who began to collect comparable statistics on the world's urban population in the mid-fifties. His first results consisted of a systematic presentation of comparative urban data for the period 1950 to 1970 (Davis, 1969). In a subsequent volume (1972), he offered some interesting statistical analyses of these same data.

It was an ambitious undertaking of the sort occasionally attempted by the United Nations Department of Social Affairs (United Nations, 1968; 1969; 1971). In the end, however, such studies offer rather meagre intellectual fare. Nothing is explained; everything remains at a descriptive level. Since the early empires, rulers have always wanted to know how many people they controlled and where they lived, and they hired census takers and demographers to count them. Davis, United Nations functionaries, and others, such as El-Badry (1965) and Chen (1973), are simply doing their job.

Demographic analysts occasionally waxed more ambitious. Focussing on entire continents (Hance, 1970), broad cultural regions (Rosser, 1972b), or individual countries (Wilkinson, 1965; Mookherjee and Morrill, 1973), they attempted to wed statistical analysis to concepts gleaned from other disciplines or, like Wingo (1967), to subject their data to highly sophisticated forms of statistical manipulation for the sake of coming to 'significant' conclusions. But, useful as these works are as a source of information, they invariably fall short of providing adequate explanations.

An attempt to break out of these desertic regions to a more comprehensive understanding of urbanization was undertaken by Friedmann, McGlynn, Stuckey, and Wu (1971; for an English version, see Friedmann, 1973b, chapter 4). This article purported to present a paradigm for the comparative study of urbanization. As their unifying structure, the authors adopted a simple core-periphery or spatial systems framework for analysis. Although their focus was primarily on national systems, they explicitly recognized that these must be interpreted in the wider context of an hierarchical system of international relations.

At whatever scale of analysis—international, national, or regional— core and periphery stand, by definition, in an asymmetrical relationship of dominance/dependency that is articulated through four major spatial processes: decision-making and control, capital flows, innovation diffusion, and migration. Corresponding to each of these processes are spatial patterns: the spatial distribution of power, systems of activity location, modernization surfaces, and settlement patterns. Urbanization is thus perceived as a complex of spatial processes and their associated patterns, although the spatial relations of power (decision-making and control) are identified as the critical process to which all others are ultimately related.

The paradigm was intended to serve primarily a heuristic purpose; it represented a sorting out of relationships rather than a 'theory' endeavouring

11

to 'account for' urbanization. In contrast to the usual paradigm in the social sciences, it suggested that the nature of these relationships in space were inherently imbalanced and conflicting. It was a dynamic, deviation-amplifying process that was being modelled.

The paradigm also brought together the various disciplines involved in the study of urbanization, including geography, sociology, political science, and economics. It was meant as a source of hypotheses that would cross-link the traditional disciplinary approaches to the study of urbanization. This hope has yet to be realized, however (Wulff, 1973b). With the important exception of Schmidt's work (1973) in South Africa, the spatial conflict model has not inspired further investigations into specific historical settings. And although the study of *international* dependency relations and their impact on national development has advanced a good bit (Frank, 1967; Stallings, 1972; Bonilla and Girling, 1973), the translation to spatial analysis has only just begun, and none of the relevant publications are yet available in English (Rofman, 1972; Coraggio, 1972, 1973; Schteingart, 1973; Stuckey, 1973–4). A very different, but potentially promising subject for investigation is that of the relationship between urbanization and political change. This is the domain of sociologists and political scientists, and the emphasis has been on the consequences of urbanization for national politics and development. It is a rapidly proliferating field of studies, but it has yet to illuminate the urbanization process itself. Failure to adopt a spatial systems framework, for example, has led to the neglect of inter-regional conflict as an area of special study and of attempted solutions to these conflicts (Soja, 1969; Friedmann, 1972–3). As McGee (1971b) has shown for Southeast Asia, core-periphery conflicts can have very major consequences for urbanization.

Finally, macro-studies of urbanization have enticed a small number of scholars to rise above disciplinary lines and to generalize from the empirical materials available, pointing to conclusions beyond the data themselves. The roots of this theorizing are in the practice of contemporary social science. But Marxist writers have begun to challenge these theories and to offer an alternative interpretation (Harvey, 1973).

We shall devote the remainder of this part to a review of these materials beginning with the four spatial processes and patterns identified in the urbanization paradigm by Friedmann *et al.* (1971).

1 Urbanization processes I: decision-making, control, and the spatial distribution of power

'The distribution of rewards in a society is a function of the distribution of power, not of system needs.' Gerhard Linski's assertion (cited in Miller, 1971b, 211) has a certain common-sense appeal, yet it is only within the last few years that we have begun to look at the evolution of urban systems in terms of both the internal and external distribution of power.[3]

This effort has been spurred by a group of Latin American social scientists some of whose writings have been brought together in a volume edited by Martha Schteingart (1973; see also Sunkel, no date; and, for Africa, Stuckey, 1973–4). A full restatement of what has come to be known as dependency theory in its application to urbanization is not possible here. Basically, it involves the notion that powerful corporate and national interests, representing capitalist society at its most advanced, established outposts in the principal cities of Third World countries for three interrelated purposes: to extract a sizeable surplus from the dependent economy, in the form of primary products, through principally a process of 'unequal exchange'; to expand the market for goods and services produced in the home countries of advanced monopoly capitalism; and to ensure stability of an indigenous political system that will resist encroachment by ideologies and social movements that threaten to undermine the basic institutions of the capitalistic system. All three forms of penetration are ultimately intended to serve the single purpose of helping to maintain expanding levels of production and consumption in the home countries of advanced capitalism.[4]

In the course of this process, local elites are co-opted. Their life style becomes imitatively cosmopolitan, and this further alienates them from the vast majority of their own people whose language they often do not even speak. The elites' ability to gather a growing proportion of the nation's wealth into their own hands forces more and more of the rural and urban masses to live and multiply close to subsistence (Economic Commission for Latin America, 1974). At the same time, the elites' own needs for consumption are met by implementing industrialization policies based on the concept of import substitution. These policies contribute to growing primacy in the distribution of city sizes, because the principal domestic market is concentrated in the city where the elites reside, and processes of 'circular and cumulative causation' (Pred, 1973a) tend to sustain accelerated growth at this location.[5] Economic spread effects are

---

[3] 'Just as power can be measured in terms of how decisions allocate benefits and burdens to groups and individuals, so power can be measured in terms of how decisions allocate benefits and burdens to different places within society. Such locational decisions refer to the assignment of certain functions, services, expenditures to individual locations or the application of certain controls, restrictions, or incentives which affect locational use' (Cadei, 1974, 20).

[4] Latest versions of this theory see the domination of peripheral economies primarily of help in the expansion of multi-national corporations that exhibit a growing independence of action from national commitments and control.

[5] Because domestic markets are limited, new import-substitution industries are gradually giving way to industries that are export-oriented. Both, however, are in large measure controlled by international corporations. A study conducted by

13

minimal and can occur only where compatible economic structures exist. Provincial cities serve primarily as administrative centres for the control of their associated regions and as points for the trans-shipment of agricultural and mineral products destined for export. The growing regional inequalities that result from this situation, coupled with a rapidly increasing peasant population, induce massive transfers of rural people to the urban enclave economy where they come to join the ranks of the marginally unemployed, producing a form of 'urbanization without industrialization' with its concomitant phenomena of 'involution' (see part IV, section 3) and 'ruralization' (see introduction to part IV).

In order to maintain political stability in the face of growing opposition to a process which envisions the incorporation of the 'underdeveloped' countries into the periphery of international capitalism, conservative military dictatorships are established under the tutelage of the American military establishment. Political opposition is eliminated, and the economy is increasingly organized to maximize the income and material wealth of the commercial–industrial–military elites who manage the economy in the interest of the international system of which they are a part.

This theory of dependency or, more accurately, of *dependent capitalism*, seems to account for certain forms of spatial development in newly industrializing societies. But a number of factors are passed over in the theory which render its stark simplicities considerably more complex. Repression alone, for example, is not enough to maintain political stability in the long run. Particularly in large and culturally heterogenous societies (India, Nigeria) and in countries with a long tradition of regional urbanism (Mexico), the pressures engendered by growing regional disparities may lead to a limited sharing of political power with subordinate spatial units (Duchacek, 1970). As a result, indices of primacy will tend to be much lower in federated or decentralized states than in unitary or highly centralized states, and the effects of economic development tend to be more equally distributed throughout the national space.[6]

---

the United States Department of Commerce indicates that about 41 per cent of the exports of manufactured products from Latin American countries in 1966 were accounted for by the local subsidiaries of United States enterprises, though the latter represented only ten per cent of total manufacturers in the area. And about 65 per cent of the $900 million increase in Latin American exports of manufactures between 1957 and 1966 originated in the local subsidiaries of United States parent companies (Biederman, 1974, 15–16). These industries typically enjoy much lower labour costs than their counterparts in the United States and so are highly competitive in international markets.

[6] The following three-city indices, calculated from national censuses for 1970, help to illustrate the relation between territorial organization and urbanization. One possible reason for the low national primacy indices in India, Nigeria, and Brazil is the large size of their respective economies which requires organization through a system of regional primate cities. Some regions in these countries may,

Such a sharing of political power (and of some of the fruits of development) is almost always the result of prior conflict between elites at the political centre and aspiring counter-elites in the periphery. These inter-regional struggles may become very severe and lead to a variety of possible outcomes that include *co-optation* of peripheral counter-elites by the centre (extension of the principle of dependent capitalism to the interior of the country); *accommodation* between central and peripheral elites by carving out mutually exclusive 'spheres of influence'; *open conflict*, including but not limited to civil war; and the establishment of *regional protectorates*, such as the 'native homelands' policy pursued by the South African government (Friedmann, 1972–3, 31–8).

Each of these outcomes implies a shift in the spatial distribution of power and, in consequence, in the spatial distribution of economic functions and in the relations among the several spatial subsystems comprising the economy. The evolution of the urban system towards greater equality in the relevant indices of development is sometimes seen as the automatic results of innovation diffusion, spread effects, or economic decisions operating in an unregulated market economy. But nothing could be further from the truth. As Rozman (1973) has shown for even pre-industrial societies, it is the *distribution of effective political and economic power* which, in the end, determines the spatial organization of an urban system and its evolution.

2 Urbanization processes II: capital flows, investments, and the location of economic activities

One of the major propositions to emerge from David Harvey's essay on the origins of cities is that 'cities are . . . created out of the mobilization,

---

indeed, be as large in area and population as any of the high-index countries. Still, the fact remains that this latter group of countries represents closed political and economic systems that are highly centralized, while the low-index countries are politically 'open', the several regional capitals are linked into a single national system of political and economic relations, and power is consequently relatively more dispersed.

Unitary or highly centralized States		*Federated or highly decentralized States*	
Thailand	12·4	Indonesia	1·2
Peru	5·3	Colombia	0·9
Philippines	4·6	Malaysia	0·9
Argentina	4·0	Brazil	0·8
Ethiopia	2·5	India	0·7
Iran	2·2	Yugoslavia	0·6
Senegal	2·2	Nigeria	0·6
U.A.R.	2·1		

extraction and geographic concentration of significant quantities of the socially designated surplus product' (Harvey, 1973, 238–9). Translated into the language of classical economics, the 'socially designated surplus product' is equal to savings, or to that part of total income which is not consumed. And if we assume a closed economy, then savings must equal capital invested. Harvey's proposition, therefore, obliges us to look at the ways in which capital is mobilized and invested to produce urban economic growth and the physical expansion of cities.

Just as a city's long-term population growth results from both natural increase and net migration, so its economic growth is spurred by capital investments from savings within the urban economy itself, from capital extracted and transferred from rural areas and other cities within the national economy, and from net capital transfers from aboard. The question of foreign capital imports was implicitly treated in the preceding section as part of our discussion of the theory of dependency; here we shall confine our attention to the transfer of capital from the internal periphery of a country to its respective core region economies. In this spatial or urban systems perspective, we shall want to know what proportion of urban investments is financed by capital transfers from the periphery, and whether this is done through private or through public channels; in what activities this surplus is invested, and where they are located; and how these processes affect the overall distribution of activities and trade patterns in space. Beyond this we shall also want to know to what extent economic spread effects occur, both down the urban hierarchy and out into the periphery of each centre; and, finally, how all of the preceding change-inducing processes affect the spatial organization of the economy and the distribution of economic welfare.

To the best of our knowledge, there are no comprehensive studies which address themselves to all of these questions for even a single Third World country, but an incomplete, synthetic picture can be pieced together from the available, if fragmentary evidence. We shall briefly address five related topics: the transfer of capital from the periphery to finance urban expansion; countervailing income transfers from urban to rural areas; the location of manufacturing industries; the question of spread effects; and the problem of interregional inequality.

a The transfer of capital from the periphery: There can be very little argument that in almost all parts of the world urban development is and has been financed, at least in its initial stages, by the mobilization of a surplus from agricultural producers (Mellor, 1973). Historically, the methods varied from country to country. But whether major reliance was placed on repressive extraction by a wealthy land-owning class, compulsive deliveries, taxation, land rents, or adverse terms of trade, the results were always the same: peasants were squeezed for the ultimate benefit of urban populations. And much of this squeeze was applied through the private sector. A United Nations study of Northern Thailand (1968), for example, reports:

> It appears that a proportion of the considerable deposits which are made in the provincial branches and agencies of the commercial banks are transferred to the head offices of the bank in Bangkok and are invested in loans and advances there. Thus, the proportion of time deposits and demand deposits which the commercial banks draw from their country branches outside Bangkok is over 45 per cent and over 37 per cent of their total time and demand deposits. As against this, less than 20 per cent of their loans and overdrafts are made in the provinces by the branches and agencies. Thus, it would appear that almost half the total deposits made in the provinces are invested in loans and advances by the Bangkok head offices. It must be assumed that this is as true of the Northern Region as of others, and that the oans and advances made by the head offices will, in their great bulk, go to firms ocated in Bangkok.

In various forms, these findings might be replicated in many other countries, such as Nigeria (Smith and Hay, 1970) and Mexico. A major exception appears to be India where, at least through the latter part of the 1960s, the net transfer of resources favoured rural areas rather than cities (Mellor, 1973, 9). This might explain India's surprisingly low rate of urban growth which was only 2·4 per cent per annum between 1950 and 1960 and 2·9 per cent in the succeeding decade (Davis, 1969, table D). As Mellor is at pains to point out, however, this favourable financial situation could not result in significantly higher rates of agricultural production so long as Indian agriculture remained technologically backward. For under these conditions, physical response was low and physical returns on capital diminished, so that the marginal efficiency of capital, but for a fortuitous rise in agricultural prices, would have been greater in alternative employments. In order to raise agricultural productivity, capital must be joined to technological innovation. This appears to have occurred with the 'green revolution' which was introduced to India less than a decade ago. But whether the overall results of this 'revolution', including its long-term social and ecological effects, are also favourable on balance, is a question on which the final evidence is not yet in.

b Income transfers from urban to rural areas: Until quite recently, little was known about the 'informal' flows of savings from urban migrants to their home districts in rural areas. This is not surprising, since these flows by-pass the commercial banking sector and can be identified, and their total volume estimated, only through anthropological field research. On the basis of such limited evidence, however, Mellor (1973, note 24) suggests that urban–rural transfers might be quite large for India. And Carlos Orellana, in his study of Mixtec migrants to Mexico

City (1973, 279), reports that the regional association (*Union Vecinal*) of migrants from a rural community near Oaxaca imposed 'the traditional *tequio* system of community obligations which is required from all migrants. . . . The stated objective of the *tequio* is to carry out improvements in the material conditions of the village.' Regional associations in Lima follow a similar practice. According to Doughty (1970, 42), 'although the average yearly contribution of one hundred eighty dollars may seem small, it is, nevertheless substantial when one considers that municipal expenditures for rural districts in Peru *averaged* about two hundred dollars a year until 1964 when the national government began to provide direct subsidies to municipalities.'

The most detailed data, however, come from a recent study in Nairobi from which the authors conclude that 'urban–rural income transfers represent about one-fifth of the urban wage bill in Kenya' (Johnson and Whitelaw, 1974, 477). It may be interesting to note that low-income migrants appeared to save a greater portion of their income for transfer to their native districts than did migrants whose incomes, on average, were larger. This surprising conclusion is consistent with findings from Latin America where a cosmopolitan 'demonstration effect' seems to reduce personal savings among high income groups in cities such as São Paulo and Caracas (Economic Commission for Latin America, 1974, 43–4).

In any event, the contributions to local rural districts may be sizeable. In 1967, over 8,000 Nigerian pounds were contributed for local use by migrants from the Western Nigerian town of Shaki (Mabogunje, 1972, 135–7). Of course, the transferred amounts were not always invested; some portion was consumed, and a good bit might be spent on education. But from the viewpoint of the family, educational expenditures might also be regarded as an investment. For education would give to one of their own kin a better chance to find a job and so perhaps, in time, enable other kinsmen to also gain a foothold in the city.

c Location of manufacturing industries: William Alonso (1971) has provided a convincing rationale why private investors would want to seek locations for manufacturing enterprise in large cities. The reasons include the physical pattern of transportation, the concentration of markets, time–distance relationships, location preferences of managers and technicians, the spatial distribution of information, the cost of time in decisions relating to location, and external economies. A look at the empirical evidence seems to confirm Alonso's thesis. In a study of manufacturing in tropical Africa, Akin Mabogunje (1973, 11) reports the following percentage distributions of manufacturing for the capital cities of 23 African countries:

18

Per cent of total Mfg. in the Capital City	Number of Countries
80–100	7
60– 79	5
40– 59	4
20– 39	6
20	1

In attempting to explain this pattern, Mabogunje refers to much the same hypotheses as Alonso: the concentration of markets, good infrastructure facilities, and high access. Moreover, many of the capital cities are also major ports for their respective countries. 'It is thus easy to appreciate,' writes Mabogunje (1973, 11), 'why industrial development in most African countries has tended to reinforce the importance of the capital city and give it a very notable primacy.'

A high degree of polarization of manufacturing employment has also been demonstrated for India (Berry, 1966). Although Brian Berry's study was primarily concerned with interregional trade patterns, he found (p. 192) that 'the fundamental spatial patterns that summarize the characteristics of areas and the types of spatial behaviour that are the essence of the interactions taking place among the areas are interdependent and basically isomorphic.' And he goes on to say (p. 239): 'India's economic system is to be viewed regionally as (*a*) an interacting set of economic activities based upon major resource complexes, together with (*b*) disaggregation into a set of regional economies oriented about major metropolitan centres. Both resource complexes and metropolitan nodes (the traditional and colonial elements of India's economy) can be associated with core regions of more intensive activity, surrounded by peripheries in which simpler peasant economies remain. The metropolitan centres serve not only as points of organization for their regional economies, but also as the points of concentration through which the main interregional commodity movements are articulated.' The principal 'growth poles' of Calcutta, Bombay, Madras, and Delhi stand out in his analysis, but an additional series of smaller centres also appears. (For similar results of a locational analysis for manufacturing in mainland China, see Wu, 1967.) It is these cities which absorb a major share of the total urban growth in the economy and, through their commercial contact networks, help organize the space economy into major core-periphery systems.

d The question of spread effects A frequently expressed assumption about so-called growth centres is that economic growth focussed upon them will eventually 'filter down' the urban hierarchy and spread out

19

from each centre into its immediate periphery. The evidence, however, is less clear than might be thought (Brown, 1974). Rural areas surrounding industrializing cities participate, if at all, to only a very limited extent in the expansion of the urban economy (Ellefson, 1962). And neither backward nor forward linkages are very strong.

The typical city has an enclave economy whose multipliers are either extremely localized or captured by metropolitan economies that control most of its 'modern' business sector (Mabogunje, 1971, 48–55; Brandt, Schubert, and Gerken, 1972). For 'spread' to occur, the structure of the rural economy must be roughly isomorphic with that of the city; it must be organized (or capable of being organized) along commercial, capitalistic lines. In addition, the periphery must be economically accessible to the core area.

These conditions are met to a very limited extent in newly industrializing countries where much of the traditional peasant agriculture still remains outside the influence of market forces. There is some tendency for economic growth to 'filter down' one or two levels of the urban hierarchy, but lower-order cities tend to respond more to demands from expanding agricultural production in their immediate hinterlands than to growth impulses from above. 'Spread effects' are therefore limited to those agricultural regions, such as in Mexico's northwest, that are closely tied into the capitalistic system by virtue of their specialization in commercial crops produced primarily for export. The indigenous food-producing sector tends to be bypassed by the expanding market economy and operates primarily through traditional channels of distribution (Thodey, 1969).

e The problem of inter-regional inequality: The review of the literature up to this point suggests that the outcome of spatial capital flows for the inter-regional distribution of per capita income would be highly uneven. And this, indeed, is by and large the case. The most comprehensive study on the subject is Jeffrey Williamson's (1965).

Williamson's well-known thesis is that regional income differences tend to grow larger during the early stages of economic development, then level off, only to decline again with the growing maturity and spatial integration of the economy. To buttress his thesis, Williamson presents comparative data for 24 countries, arranged in groups from high to low per capita incomes. A smaller number of countries is subjected to time series analysis. In both cases, his calculations do indeed yield the expected values. Very poor and large countries, such as India, have relatively low indices of inequality; countries on the 'middle rung', such as Brazil and Colombia, exhibit the most extreme forms of inequality; whereas the top group of countries—Australia, New Zealand, Canada, the United Kingdom, United States, and Sweden—show very low measures of regional income dispersion. Similar results are obtained for time series data pertaining to individual countries. Williamson regards this as a necessary and essential process for 'successful' development. His article has therefore been frequently cited in support of inherently *inegalitarian* spatial policies. For why should a country endeavour to produce more equal patterns of economic welfare through programmes of industrial decentralization and agricultural development if such measures run counter to the grand scheme of history and sacrifice essential growth for the dubious advantages of greater social justice (Mera, 1973)?

But there are a number of difficulties with Williamson's analysis which, except for one, have been largely overlooked by regional economists. Aside from the questionable validity of his principal measure of dispersion (Metwally and Jensen, 1973), there is the controversial assumption that countries can be meaningfully aligned along a single dimension of 'successful' development (i.e., per capita income). Even more to the point is the fact that the time period required for the reduction of regional inequalities through the operation of 'spontaneous' market forces might take a century or longer, and even then, at presumably high levels of urbanization, industrialization, and per capita incomes, interregional differences might still be cause for widespread agitation. But most important of all, from a standpoint of public policy, is the fact that the *absolute* differences in per capita income and other welfare measures may be politically more significant than the relative measure of income dispersion on which his analysis is based—a point which Williamson concedes. Perhaps he is right, and capitalistic systems generate long-term cycles in the interregional dispersion of income, so that convergence upon a mean eventually occurs. But this is small consolation for the policy maker for whom gross spatial inequalities, *whose absolute values are increasing*, remain a daily fact of life throughout his entire political career.

3 Urbanization processes III: the spatial diffusion of innovations and patterns of modernization

The concept of spatial diffusion is closely related to that of spread effect which was briefly touched upon in the preceding section. Spread effects may be mapped by measuring the results of a prior diffusion of innovations in terms of selected socio-economic indices. The resulting spatial contours are sometimes referred to as a 'modernization surface' (Soja and Tobin, 1974). If we accept this distinction, the adoption of innovations may be seen as the leading influence on the spatial incidence of economic development and of changes in customary modes of living.

Research in spatial innovation diffusion has made major contributions to our understanding of the dynamics of urban systems growth and distribution. But relatively few diffusion studies have focussed on what we have called the urban transition in newly industrializing countries.

The study of innovation diffusion is concerned with explaining the processes leading to the differential adoption of particular innovations in a time-space framework. Some but not all of these innovations are material in inducing urban growth. A simple classification may help to draw these distinctions more sharply.

Growth-related innovations may be called *entrepreneurial*. The 'adopting' unit in this instance is a formal organization, such as a business enterprise, a farm production unit, or governmental agency. Some confusion may result from the fact that the introduction of an entrepreneurial innovation to a spatially defined local community is often the planned result of a decision by a non-local parent organization, for example, a national Ministry of Health that locates a rural health clinic in a particular district. An innovation is always spatially defined, but in this instance, the health clinic would not be 'adopted' by the local community so much as 'imposed' upon it by the Ministry to which it had been introduced earlier in the nation's capital.

In any event, entrepreneurial innovations may be further subdivided into *growth-supporting* and *growth-inducing* innovations. The former include all innovations that are normally included under the rubric of socio-economic infrastructure, while the latter refers to directly productive activities. In addition, however, growth-related innovations may refer to new forms of organizing traditional economic and social activities (for example, the reorganization of local retail trade through supermarkets) as well as to new techniques for producing goods and services (for example, the introduction of new machine technology or of new agricultural implements, such as tractors).

Non-growth-related innovations, on the other hand, are exclusively confined to the adoption of new consumer goods and services by individual households. Most diffusion research has concentrated on these *consumer innovations*, partly because of the ease with which they lend themselves to statistical treatment and perhaps also because the adoption of consumer innovations figures importantly in the demand-led growth of the advanced industrial economies where most of the research has been conducted. But whatever the reason, we shall ignore this type of innovation in the discussion which follows and concentrate instead on growth-related and, more particularly, on growth-inducing innovations.

A further useful distinction relates to the scale of observation. Brown and Lentnek suggest a division into three relevant scales (1973, 274–5): a *macroscale* which refers to diffusion through the urban system as a whole, a *mesoscale* for focusing on diffusion within the hinterland of a single urban centre, and a *microscale* at which the adoption process within a single small community or highly localized rural area is examined. Because of its relevance for urban system growth, only the literature relating to the diffusion of entrepreneurial innovations at the macroscale will be considered in the present context.

Attempts to formulate a general theory relating innovation diffusion to the growth of urban systems have been undertaken by Lasuén (1971), Berry (1972), Hermansen (1972), Friedmann (1972; 1972–3; 1973a); and Pred (1973a; 1973b). But, in so far as these theories refer to the urbanization experience of newly industrializing countries, they have drawn extensively on a small number of empirical studies for Kenya (Soja, 1968), Chile (Pedersen, 1970), Sierra Leone (Riddell, 1970), and Tanzania (Gould, P. R., 1970). Highly original in their own right, each of these studies contributes special insights into the processes of city formation, modernization, and spatial integration. Yet they are all conceptually deficient in that they fail to make the distinctions among the several types of innovation which we feel are essential for a deeper understanding of the processes involved.

In spite of these shortcomings, there is considerable agreement in the empirical findings. Soja's early formulation for Kenya (1968, 101) may be allowed to stand: 'The impact of modernization was therefore highly uneven. Traditional social and economic organization, pre-European patterns of migration, and, perhaps most importantly, *geographic proximity and accessibility to the major nodes and flow lines within the new circulation system* affected the degree to which various peoples of Kenya were exposed to and transformed by the processes of change.'

The extent of unevenness in the 'modernization surface' is particularly well illustrated by Gould's research on Tanzania (1970; for a comparison with Sierra Leone, see Soja and Tobin, 1974). A careful look at his distributions, spanning the period from 1920 to 1963, not only reveals an impressive stability of spatial patterns over time, but also the enormous differences existing in the indices of 'modernization' between the capital region of Dar es Salaam and other cities and towns along the major 'space-bridging' transportation routes of the country. If the composite index of 'modernization' for Tanzania's principal core area is set equal to 1,000, only ten other urban places had indices of 200 and above in 1963 (compared to 8 in 1920), and the indices for the four leading centres had less than half the value for the principal core (1970, 167). In contrast, the rest of the country was barely touched by the changes incorporated into Gould's statistical measure, although there is some evidence that weak 'spread effects' tended to occur in the immediate vicinity of the more important cities.

23

In order to grasp why the kind of urban primacy observed in countries such as Tanzania occurs, it may be instructive to follow the diffusion process for a major growth-inducing innovation. The first adoption of this hypothetical innovation, such as a modern banking enterprise or manufacturing plant, is most likely to occur in the most cosmopolitan city of the country which is frequently also the nation's capital. And in all probability, it will be a foreign-controlled investment.

There are several reasons why the first adoption will tend to be in the country's major city, including the concentration of foreign residents, existing contact networks with foreign metropolitan centres, good external communications, a high level of demand for the innovation in question, a good supporting infrastructure of public and private facilities representing earlier cycles of innovation diffusion, and a cultural environment that is more or less receptive to the innovation.

The question now arises whether this first adoption will not lead to subsequent adoptions of the same innovation. The probability of this occurring will depend on a number of conditions, the most important of which is the *scale* of the innovation in question. For many types of innovation, the economic conditions in the country will permit of only *one* adoption; such innovations may be called *national*. For other innovations, a second and even third round of adoption may be economically feasible, but whether they will in fact 'filter down' the hierarchy of urban centres may depend on such elements as the size of the regional market to be served, conditions of internal transport, the existence of a growth-supporting infrastructure in the locality, a benign cultural environment, etc. In general, however, since the relevant innovation represents a foreign invention adapted to the conditions of relative factor scarcity and economies of scale in the country of its origin, its threshold size will tend to rise with time, so that, within the adopting country, it will more often than not turn out to be either a national or regional innovation. Should it be the former, subsequent adoptions will *not* take place, and if the latter, the innovation will, in principle, be restricted to regional cities one or two levels down the urban hierarchy. By the same reasoning, all lower-order centres are unlikely to receive the innovation.

Finally, one may ask whether the innovation initially adopted in the principal city will not tend to 'generate' a demand for related innovations. To some extent, this may in fact occur, although the probability is high that interrelated clusters of innovations will occur at the points most accessible to the initial adoption and thus again within the core and for very much the same reasons as those which accounted for the first innovation itself. Non-local, but national multipliers are relatively rare occurrences, except as the original innovation wishes to assure itself of a continuing flow of resources from the periphery. In that case, subsidiary innovations such as branch banks, may be 'implanted' at strategically selected points. Only innovations which are extremely fungible such as bottling plants, dry cleaning establishments, and raw material processing industries, may finally reach down the urban hierarchy to fairly 'local' levels. And to some extent the same will be true for certain items of urban infrastructure, such as schools, hospital clinics, water works, post offices, telephones, and cinemas which, except for the last, are usually provided by the government itself. In all these cases, urban hierarchy and relative accessibility will tend to be decisive (Riddell, 1970, 43–93), although the additional question of cultural receptivity should not be dismissed as unimportant (Morse, 1970a).

As useful as the literature on spatial innovation diffusion has been for explaining urban growth, especially when diffusion processes have been linked to migration (Riddell, 1970), it has done little more than 'certify' the large-city-focussed model of spatial development (Pred, 1973a, chapter 4). The process described gives rise not only to major regional imbalances (see discussion in the preceding section) but also to the mushrooming growth of the 'informal' employment sector and to the housing problems associated with it in the principal cities of a country (see IV for further discussion of these issues). In view of these results, one may question the utility of the diffusion model as a *prescriptive base* for spatial development policy (Harvey and Greenberg, 1972).

Typically, the growth-inducing innovations studied are complex innovations that are imported *in their entirety* and grafted unto a traditional economy with very little modification. Most of their multipliers are non-local and have their major incidence abroad. Thus it was a relatively easy matter for the United States to cripple Chilean industry during the Allende period by simply shutting off the supply flow of spare parts vital for industrial 'innovations' which had been previously introduced and adopted by that country. Moreover, rising capital coefficients and scale economies of imported technology tend to make each round of innovation less capable of downward diffusion. This contributes to urban primacy and accentuates incipient economic dualism in the adopting country. Furthermore, it leaves the country technologically dependent, encourages monopolistic practices, introduces an important factor of economic and political vulnerability, and prevents economic development from becoming the major learning process that it should be (Dunn, 1971).

Under these conditions, growth centre policies are likely to fail in all but the most exceptional circumstances (see Part V). A hand-me-down process of 'century-skipping' which is ultimately controlled from abroad and incorporates newly industrializing countries as the more or less passive periphery of world core regions is unlikely to bring the benefits desired. As difficult as it may be, only a self-reliant, autonomous form of development based on native ingenuity in small-scale production, carefully mixed with foreign technology on a highly selective basis, may be capable of producing a well-articulated, integrated space economy.

This was essentially the way in which the now 'advanced' economies developed when they themselves were newly industrializing. It would be very odd, indeed, if the principles that we have learned from the urban history of Europe and the United States should now be suddenly replaced by a whole new set that virtually ignores that experience.

4 Urbanization processes IV: migration and settlement

As the most visible and dramatic phenomenon in the growth of cities, migration is sometimes confounded with the very essence of urbanization itself. Under rapid urban expansion, migrants may account for up to 75 per cent of the total increase in major city populations,[7] and the number of temporary sojourners may be still larger. Internal migration is thus a subject of never-ending fascination (Kuper, H., 1965; Balán, Browning, and Jelin, 1973; Harris and Weiner, 1973). Students of comparative urbanization are likely to forget, however, that migration to cities reflects merely a demographic adjustment to changes in the spatial structure of economic and social opportunities that result from the major urbanization processes already discussed: the exercise of power, capital movements, and innovation diffusion. Migration is a *derived phenomenon*, a symptom of urbanization and not the thing itself.

But it is also a universal and, to all appearances, uni-directional and irreversible phenomenon. It would thus appear to be man's fate to live in cities. The only question is what form the cities shall take and under what conditions man shall make his home in them.

[7] The World Bank (1972, Annex I, Table 4) reports the following percentage contributions of migrants to urban growth:

	Period	Per cent
Abidjan	1955–63	76
Bogota	1955–66	33
Bombay	1961–61	52
Caracas	1950–60	54
Djakarta	1961–68	59
Istanbul	1950–60	68
Lagos	1952–62	75
Nairobi	1961–69	50
São Paulo	1950–60	72
	1960–67	68
Seoul	1955–65	63
Taipei	1950–60	40
	1960–67	43

The long-term, continuing movement to cities implies the ascendancy of a type of economy where only a small proportion of the population will eventually engage in farming (Jacobson and Prakash, 1971b). Because industry was understood to be the leading sector in this transformation, the growing discrepancy in the number of available jobs in manufacturing and the size of the urban working force has caused widespread concern with 'over-urbanization' (Sovani, 1964). But the connection to the type of industrialization that produced this discrepancy and the reasons for it (i.e., dependent capitalism) failed to be made. Instead, politicians, social scientists, and planners worried about how to reduce the steady stream of migrants to the city.

Although the effort was quite hopeless—the economic system was after all designed to generate this movement—it produced a large number of studies on migration, a vast accumulation of data, and very little insight into what was really happening. Demographers and others insisted on treating migration as a major policy variable when it was, in fact, dependent on the major structural features of the economy. Or more directly: unless these features were to change, the established pattern of migration would simply reproduce itself.

Although a theory of urban development that would incorporate migration did not emerge, with the possible exception of Samir Amin's work (1972), a modest number of conclusions may be drawn from the massive literature. The generality of these conclusions cannot be vouchsafed, however, and for each and every one of them there are bound to be significant exceptions. Yet short of summarizing all the extant studies and codifying their results—truly a Herculean task—there exists no other way of saying anything intelligent about migration that is not tied to a specific country. And so, conclusions must be risked.

1   Although the potential migrant is always an individual or a small family unit, the decision to migrate is frequently collective, involving members of the extended kinship group and occasionally of the rural community as a whole (Wilkie, 1968; Caldwell, 1969).
2   The group making the decision does so rationally on the basis of direct, personal information concerning economic and social opportunities in the target city relative to equivalent opportunities perceived to exist at home (Caldwell, 1969).
3   Fairly stable perceptions of residential desirability and hence of potential migrant vectors are formed during early adolescence (Gould and Ola, 1970).
4   Migrants tend to come in proportionately larger numbers from densely populated areas that are in frequent contact with the city. This includes all of the city's immediate surroundings, but also areas that

27

abut on major transportation corridors and are at least to some degree incorporated into the market economy whose transactions are focused and controlled by the city (Balán, 1969; Rivière d'Arc, 1973, 95–106).

5 Migrants are positively selected from their home populations for such characteristics as age, marital status, sex, education, and family income (Herrick, 1965; Caldwell, 1969; Zachariah, 1969). Thus it is not the most poorly but the best endowed who tend to migrate to the city. Over time, however, the degree of selectivity may regress towards the mean in the distribution of the relevant variables pertaining to the migrants' home communities (Browning and Feindt, 1969).

6 The migrant moves in what may be called a spatially extended social field through which he maintains steady contact with his kin, tribal group, or home community and which, in turn, is held together by a network of reciprocal obligations (Abu-Lughod, 1961; Lambert, 1962; Little, 1965; Gutkind, 1965; Cohen, 1969; Doughty, 1970; Hollnsteiner, 1972; Orellana, 1973; Weisner, 1973; Heisler, 1974). This may be somewhat less true of Latin American migrants, however, whose rural communities are less well organized and often much more transitory than those in Africa and Southeast Asia (Morse, 1970b).

7 Migrants tend to move in a step-wise, upward progression along the urban hierarchy, but direct migration from rural areas in the vicinity of cities also occurs (Herrick, 1965; Arriaga, 1968; Riddell and Harvey, 1972). In parts of tropical Africa, however, migration often proceeds by a sharp 'leap' from small village to distant urban centre (Epstein, A. L., 1967).

8 Not all moves to the city are permanent. Among the temporary forms of rural–urban migration the following types have been singled out for attention: reverse migration (Feindt and Browning, 1972; Zachariah, 1969), circular migration (Elkan, 1967), and floating migration (Breeze, 1966, 83). On balance, however, the gain in urban population from migration is always positive.

Important as it is in a quantitative sense, the type of rural to urban migration described in these eight propositions is not the only one. It simply happens to be a social phenomenon which, because of its regularity and persistence, has been studied in detail. But there are also significant migrations which result from war and environmental disaster, such as soil exhaustion, droughts, flooding, and locust invasions (McGee, 1971b; Hance, 1970, 166–76). Migrations that have their origin in these conditions might more properly be called 'displacements'.

Although the entire urban system shares in the migratory movements discussed above, individual cities do not do so equally, and the terminal point is always a major core region. It is here that the structure of opportunities is perceived to be greatest.

In Africa, core areas are also the principal producing centres for export, and the labour economy of the entire continent is organized in terms of them. (In the case of countries like Morocco and Algeria, the relevant core regions are located in Western Europe.) Each major core has a multinational periphery from which its labour supply is drawn (Hance, 1970, 147). Except in a few cases, therefore, national boundaries do not act as significant barriers between the peripheries of adjacent countries, though in recent years some governments have taken measures to reduce the flow of foreign migrants (Mabogunje, 1972, chapter 4).

A good deal of empty controversy has agitated academic minds concerning the 'true causes' of migration. Everett Lee's theory (1966) of contending 'push' and 'pull' factors is still quite popular in sociological accounts, though economic explanations are beginning to gain favour (Todaro, 1971). The usual procedure has been to ask migrants about the reasons for 'their' move, which assumes, of course, that it was the migrants' autonomous decision in the first place. (For the opposite assumption, see proposition 1 above.) A typical response for migrants to Bogotá in Colombia yields these explanations:

1 economic reasons
2 *la violencia*
3 quality of education in the rural area
4 poor health services in the rural area
5 military service
6 better living conditions in the city (Flinn, 1966)

Two things may be inferred from the replies: first, the abysmal neglect suffered by rural areas at the hands of the governing authorities in Colombia, and second, the expressed hope on the migrants' part that life would somehow be better in the nation's capital. In light of this summary interpretation, one cannot help but wonder whether the neglect of rural areas was not an intended result of benefit primarily to those for whom the migrants ultimately had to work. No more than those of any other city, elites in Bogotá are not particularly known for their altruistic feelings towards peasants.

The social, political and economic correlates of continuing rural to urban migration are many and have been the subject of extended study. The relevant literature will be reviewed under the general heading of micro-studies in part IV. One aspect, however, belongs still in the present context and concerns the relationship of urbanization to political change. It is to this topic that we now turn.

5   Urbanization and political change

One may question whether the relationship between urbanization and political change is a legitimate subject for study. The pertinent literature is rather 'thin', and within political science itself, no specialized field has yet emerged which addresses itself primarily to the mutual influences of urbanization and political change upon each other. Nor, indeed, does there exist an agreed-upon paradigm to focus researchers' attention on the critical processes involved. The closest thing to such a paradigm is Karl Deutsch's early and seminal piece on political and social integration (1953), but it has not been followed up.

The significance of a subject depends entirely on the questions that are asked of it. One problem with the present topic is that both of its related terms are aggregated to a degree that renders meaningful statement concerning their relationship extremely difficult. To most political scientists, urbanization is simply a statistic that describes the percentage of the total population living in urban places defined by some minimum threshold of population. They rarely understand it as a spatial process (but see Weiner, 1971, for a notable exception). Finally, few political scientists have looked on urbanization as a process of socio-cultural change that may proceed *outwards* from given urban centres to encroach upon rural and small-town populations in a kind of 'creeping urbanism'.[8] The more notable exceptions are the work of Lerner (1958) and Szyliowicz (1966) on Turkey, Diaz (1966) on Mexico, and Guyot (1969) on Malaysia.

Given a proper conceptual framework, however, a number of highly challenging questions may be raised and, in fact, have been occasionally addressed by the individual scholar. The following may be taken as a partial listing of such topics for research.

1   The accelerated growth of cities implies not only a shift in the distribution of power from rural to urban areas but also the appearance of entirely new social classes, among them the proto-proletariat, factory workers, and urban elites. What are the consequences of these changes in demographic and social composition for the political life of the country?

2   With the appearance of a national system of cities, implying some degree of spatial interdependency, the concept of nation begins to

[8] Social scientists distinguish between *urbanization* in the sense of demographic concentration in 'cities' and *urbanism* as a 'way of life'. The latter is assumed to be confined to life in cities and is described as a form of conditioned behaviour rather than as a process of change. It is this static notion of urbanism which has prevented most students of cities to consider urbanization as a spatial process. Geographers were the first to discover the inherent usefulness of studying this process (Soja, 1968), but their work has largely been ignored by other social scientists.

compete with traditional concepts of tribal and/or regional identification and loyalty. New national symbols are created, resources are nationally mobilized, and their allocation is for the first time regarded as a national problem. How does the manner in which this problem is resolved affect the future of urbanization and spatial organization in the country, and what are the political processes by which allocative decisions are made and carried out?

3   The process of urbanization tends to engender a typical core-periphery structure of economic and political relations which may be simple or complex, excessively 'primate' or reasonably balanced. In this view, core region elites dominate and extend their control over populations living in the periphery, and this tends to give rise to interregional conflicts that are often exacerbated by separate historical identities. What forms do these conflicts take, and how are they resolved?

4   The transition to a fully urbanized society leads through what Fred Riggs (1964) has called a 'prismatic' society that is variously characterized by a new syncretism of social forms, cultural and economic dualism, and the temporal and spatial interpenetration of old and new social arrangements. One instance of this is the emergence of a politics in which the tendency to perceive a problem primarily in ethnic terms (wherever ethnicity is a salient aspect of society) contends with one in which it is perceived more in accord with the interests of social class. How does this ambiguity in perception reveal itself in the process and how does it affect the decisions that are made? In particular, does the apparent prevalence of an ethnic politics reduce the capacity of under-privileged urban groups to make effective demands upon the political system (Hanna and Hanna, 1971, chapters 8 and 9)?

5   The appearance and growing importance of urban economic sectors in a traditional agrarian society may lead to political clashes on the basis of sectoral interests, with commercial and industrial groups arrayed on one side and those representing landed interests on the other. How are these clashes manifested on the national scene, and what consequences do they have for the future of urbanization and urban policy in the country (Mamalakis, 1969; Merkx, 1969; Friedmann, 1973b, chapter 5)?

6   The extension of urban concepts for organizing the traditional agrarian sector may lead to an erosion of 'pastoral' politics and its substitution by a more demand-oriented urban politics (Guyot, 1969). How common is this process, and what are its consequences for political and bureaucratic behaviour?

This is by no means an exhaustive list, but it serves to illustrate how a dynamic or developmental view of urbanization and political change may give occasion to a host of challenging questions for research. Political scientists, more inclined to pay attention to the micro-politics of individual cities than to the larger societal processes that form their context, have not yet found these questions to be worthy of sustained interest.

Three reasons may be advanced for this indifference. First, until recently, many political scientists (for example, Nelson, 1969; Rabinovitz, 1969) were chiefly interested in pursuing the hypothesis that accelerated urban growth in Third World countries would threaten their political stability (Tangri, 1962). When this turned out to be an improbable conjecture in face of all the evidence collected, other scholars lost interest in urbanization as an 'explanatory variable'. Second, most political scientists concerned with questions of 'modernization' and 'political development' preferred to take the nation as their basic unit of observation and to work with the concept of a spatially undifferentiated political system (for example, Nettl, 1967). And finally, the main current of political science, at least in the United States, continues to show a strong preference for the use of rigorous statistical methods and consequently relies on a form of structural analysis which, in the nature of things, is incapable of yielding significant results for the study of urbanization.

This last point is so important, it calls for further comment. Studies such as Nie's *et al.* (1969), Rabinovitz's (1969), Cameron's *et al.* (1972), and Owen and Witton's (1973) were often excessively empiricist. Generally confined to data for but a single census year, their efforts terminated in a futile search for what one is inclined to call majestic social laws. But whether multiple correlation or factor analysis was used, their statistical base was always far too weak to reveal anything other than uncertain probabilities. Moreover, none of the authors was more than superficially acquainted with the countries they studied and were consequently unable to interpret their statistical findings in light of historical circumstances. Averse to causal and even systems analysis, they tended to assign only low explanatory powers to 'urbanization'. Once they had pointed to the low r^2 of their correlations, they tended to let matters rest.

This criticism has to be understood in relation to an alternative methodology in which process and not structure tends to be emphasized. Typical studies here were carried out within a single country (but sometimes also within the context of a larger cultural region, such as Latin America or Black Africa) by writers who had actually spent considerable time abroad and so were able to go beyond the stark simplicities reported in a census. Their studies were often redolent with fascinating insights, but there was little follow-up on the hypotheses they generated in the course of their work.

To illustrate the nature of these hypotheses, an example may be drawn from Guyot's work on Malaysia (1969, 125):

My forecast is the passing of the pastoral stage of politics among the Malays. In pastoral politics the Malay voter demands of government only that it exercise authority, maintain the Sultan, defend the faith, and curb the Chinese should they stray from the pursuit of money into the political realm. The passing of this stage will be facilitated by rural development programs in which rural folk are organized and urbanized in order to receive economic benefits more efficiently. A consequence of such organization will be the firm establishment of expectations and demands for further benefits and the conversion of local political organizations from vote delivering devices into competitive markets in which political commodities (votes government benefits) are traded. Such competitive politics will probably reduce the highly centralized and responsible control of the party held by the current generation of leaders.

The many provocative ideas of others with similar methodological commitments can be mentioned only in passing. Mamalakis (1969) and Merkx (1969), for instance, explored their theory of 'sectoral clashes' with respect to Chile and Argentina. Horowitz (1967) followed the traces of class politics and internal colonialism in Latin America as a whole. Ward (1960) contrasted rural with urban political attitudes in Japan. And Friedmann (1973b, chapter 5), focusing on what he called a 'crisis of inclusion' among the urban and political masses of Chile, a crisis which he traced to accelerated urban growth, speculated about the variety of alternative outcomes for Chile's political system.

All of these studies looked at ways by which urbanization might be said to influence political processes within a country. But a subcategory of process-studies turned this relationship around and looked at the political 'feedback' of urbanization on evolving spatial patterns via national policies for urban development (see also V). Among others, these systems-analytic studies include Weiner's path-breaking essay on political demography (1971) with reference primarily to India, Goodman's investigations (1971, 1973) of ethnic politics in Southeast Asia and its effects on urban policy, the treatment of a similar subject by Hanna and Hanna (1971) for Black Africa, and Cohen's new book on the politics of urban development in the Ivory Coast (1974).

Process studies have taught us what to look for in studies of comparative urbanization. They have also contributed to our understanding of the dynamics of spatial development in specific countries. But the important tasks of further probing and comparing, and of venturing strong hypotheses concerning the relationship between urbanization and political change still lie ahead.

6 General theory of urbanization

How does one begin to theorize about urbanization as a macro-process? What is the appropriate viewpoint? And what are the relevant concepts?

It would seem that one needs to put some psychological distance between the observer and his object in order to get at any theory at all. As distinct from special theories about particular aspects of urbanism and ultimately fruitless controversies about the differences between urban and rural society, western experience has so far failed to generate an encompassing theory of urbanization, perhaps because we are still too close to the pertinent facts to see them in a meaningful perspective, or perhaps because the western social scientist, with his historical agnosticism, is incapable of grasping a process that, in its essence, is historical (Reissman, 1964). To acquire this capacity, he would either have to wed his scientific interests with a *penchant* for history or to remove himself to newly urbanizing countries where the historical process appears to proceed at a heightened speed and thus to be compressed in time.

These requirements came together in the three authors who might be said to have initiated the search for a general theory of urbanization: Bertram Hoselitz, Robert Redfield, and Milton Singer. Hoselitz, a displaced Viennese economic historian teaching at the University of Chicago, was the first to look at urbanization in the context of national economic development and thus provided an extremely useful new perspective (Hoselitz, 1960, chapter 7; original publication dated 1953). And Redfield and Singer were both anthropologists who not only had spent many years studying non-western societies but had a strong historical intuition as well.

In 1954, Hoselitz organized a conference at the University of Chicago which produced a large number of seminal pieces for the study of urbanization. One of them, co-authored by Redfield and Singer (1954), proposed to dichotomize cities into centres of *orthogenetic* and *heterogenetic transformation*. Put simply, the former were pre-industrial cities and the loci of a Great Tradition. Japanese cities of the Tokugawa era might serve as an example. It was the authors' contention that, in the global sweep of western civilization, orthogenetic cities would eventually have to give way to cities of heterogenetic transformation as, indeed, ancient Edo had yielded to Tokyo. The civilization of industrial capitalism would thus emerge triumphant in all parts.

Hoselitz's contribution to the conference was yet another pair of concepts. He wished to distinguish between *generative* and *parasitic* cities (1960, chapter 8). By the former he meant cities that contributed to economic growth in the region or country in which they were located, while by the latter he referred to those that had the opposite effect. And he continued: 'If we apply this definition to the classification of cities which Redfield and Singer present, we must conclude that cities of heterogenic transformation tend to generate cultural change, whereas cities of orthogenetic transformation tend to limit, and in the extreme, may fully impede cultural change. But this does not mean that ortho-genetic cities are necessarily parasitic with regard to economic growth. The process of primary urbanization, though leading to a reinforcement, of existing cultural patterns, may be generative of economic growth, and, at the same time, it is thinkable that cities in certain stages of secondary urbanization may exert an unfavourable effect upon economic growth of the wider geographical unit of which they form a part' (Hoselitz, 1960, 188).

Despite the reservation expressed in the last sentence, it is clear that Hoselitz thought of cities of heterogenetic transformation as prime movers in developmental change. Wishing to emphasize their positive, construc-tive role in economic growth, he called them generative cities, though parasitism was admitted as a theoretical possibility. The concept also suggested that change processes in rural society could be properly under-stood only in relation to the cities that engendered them. More to the point, traditional peasant economies would be transformed by the pene-tration of the spirit of capitalism into a countryside that was both in-fluenced and ultimately dominated by the city.

Brilliant as it was, this formulation raised more questions than it answered. For the designation of a city as 'generative' led one to ask who benefited from its impact. If one followed David Harvey (1973, 238–9), all cities might, in fact, be parasitical. Rather than generating growth for the 'wider geographical unit of which they form a part', they would generate it only for themselves and, more accurately, for those elites who controlled the means for extracting the designated surplus from every-body else in the society.

Fourteen years passed before yet another attempt was made to wrestle with the question of the role of cities in economic growth. At a conference at Jahuel, Chile, Friedmann (1973b, 167–88) presented an open systems model of urbanization. His paper was infused with a planner's optimism and laid out a scenario of what would happen if a country would success-fully traverse the path from 'narrow impact of urban life styles to total immersion in urbanism'. In Friedmann's formulation, cities were organ-izers of economic, cultural, and political space. They were also centres of innovation, environments of opportunity, and seedbeds of democratic change. The progressive development of a system of cities would further lead from imbalanced to balanced spatial systems, from urban enclaves to the complete modernization of the national society, and from partial to total spatial integration. All in all, it was a happy view based on the premise that 'underdeveloped' countries would want to be 'developed', in the sense of becoming more autonomous, more affluent, more partici-pant, and more spatially integrated national societies (169).

The basic theses of the paper came under severe attack by Richard

Morse (1971a) who, drawing on his deep historical knowledge of Latin America, undercut with biting irony the professional optimism of the planner. A rejoinder by Friedmann (1971) closed the debate for the moment but managed to raise the larger question of whether a theory of urbanization was, indeed, possible and, if it was, what form it might take.

In a sense, the Jahual Seminar carried the line of thinking begun by Hoselitz, Redfield, and Singer to its logical conclusion. The tombstone to this kind of theorizing was perhaps set by J. R. Lasuén who tried to demonstrate how the process of innovation diffusion would inevitably lead to a spatial equilibrium in economic development and the distribution of urban populations (Lasuén, 1971). This *reductio ad absurdum* of the western model which seemed to negate the possibilities of historical change, foreclosed further investigation in the context of the traditional paradigm. A new voice was badly needed.[9]

Terry G. McGee responded to the call. A geographer from New Zealand who had spent many years working in Southeast Asia, McGee did not assume, as Hoselitz and Friedmann had done, that heterogenetic cities were, on the whole, more likely to be generative of economic growth than parasitic. On the contrary, he wrote (1971a, 31) that 'in the context of the majority of the Third World countries, it seems that a theoretical framework which regards the city as the prime catalyst of change must be disregarded. And further, that to understand the role of cities properly, 'one must investigate the condition of underdevelopment which characterizes these countries, of which the cities are only a part.' In contrast to Friedmann's optimism, McGee played pessimist and saw the Third World (primate) city as parasitical on the populations in its periphery.

His major contribution, however, was a theory of urban involution (McGee, 1971a, chapter 3). Focussing on a sectoral model of the urban economy, he rendered the basic core-periphery relationship more acceptable by explicitly introducing the concept of dependent capitalism. This he superimposed upon what he called, borrowing a concept from Clifford Geertz, the bazaar economy or the indigenous, labour-intensive sector of urban production. It was in this sector that an endless process of proliferating work occurred primarily to serve the growing population in this sector and the peasant economy with which it stood in a relation of reciprocal exchange. According to McGee, capitalist enterprise would tend to squeeze both the bazaar and the peasant economies, pushing

---

[9] It should be added that these conclusions did not become immediately apparent. Friedmann's own work on polarized development and core-periphery relationships (1973b, Part I) as well as on the territorial organization of power (1972–3) seemed to point beyond equilibrium to more dynamic possibilities that did not necessarily exclude the possibility of revolutionary transformation.

surplus rural labour into cities while, at the same time, reducing the productive capabilities of the bazaar in competition with the corporate sector. If this process of capitalist penetration could be contained, a possibility he clearly entertained, involution might yet continue for some time. But if it could not, then the growing immiseration of the urban proto-proletariat would eventually lead to pressures for revolutionary change (or, alternatively, one might add, to the imposition of a military dictatorship of the politically dominant bourgeoisie, shored up by foreign capitalist powers). The model of pre-revolutionary Cuba was held up as a case in point. In Cuba, according to McGee, the bazaar and peasant economies had been so eviscerated by capitalist penetration that, faced with famine and chronic unemployment on a massive scale, the proto-proletariat brought into being the first socialist society in the New World.

In order further to elaborate this model, it will be necessary to follow David Harvey's admonition (1973, 240) to analyse 'the processes which create, mobilize, concentrate and manipulate the social product'. In short, it will be necessary to carry out a full-scale Marxist analysis of contemporary urbanization. Whether, in fact, one does so will depend on whether one believes dependent capitalism capable of developing a country's economy within a democratic framework and thus avoiding the dire consequences predicted by McGee. Unfortunately, the current Third World situation gives little ground for hope that a just and free society can be achieved through planned reform.

IV Micro-studies of urban life

We may define a city as a spatially organized subsystem of society. Micro-studies of urban life seek to describe and explain the processes and structures of these subsystems and analyse the relationship they bear to the larger social wholes of which they form a part.

Unfortunately, we lack a heuristic paradigm within the social sciences that would permit us explicitly to link these micro-studies with the emerging paradigms for the study of urbanization as a macro-process. As a result, we have no guidelines to help us identify a relevant focus for research, sort out the significant observations from all those that are possible, pose questions that are relevant for the study of urbanization, and suggest transdisciplinary generalizations about urban life.

The typical method in micro-studies is the case study. But this immediately raises the fundamental question: case of what? Unless this question can be answered satisfactorily, nothing can be inferred from the case study beyond the immediate data themselves. Cities differ from each other along many significant dimensions, but there is no single, generally accepted typology of cities that would help maintain some comparability among the observations made. On *a priori* grounds, one would expect observational data to vary with the size of city, its economic functions, its historical evolution, its stage of technological development, its recent rate of demographic growth, its social composition, and its relative location within a larger network of information-exchange. Most so-called case studies of urban life fail to place their data into the appropriate 'boxes' of a matrix that would control for these variables. And the planners and politicians who use the results of these studies in their work tend to do so indiscriminately, without allowing for the severe limitations imposed on their validity by the restricted nature of their empirical base.

An even more serious limitation arises from the fact that urban studies concern life in spatially organized *subsystems* of larger societies. The extent to which the life of cities reflects these encompassing influences is rarely considered. To what extent are the cities in question exposed to the influences of dependent capitalism (for example, Lagos) or to an autonomous form of socialism (for example, Tangshan) (Baker, 1973; Lewis, 1971b)? What is the Great Tradition in which they share and for which they may, in fact, be centres of 'orthogenetic' transformation (Redfield, 1953; Redfield and Singer, 1954)?

One popular notion has it that cities in the Third World are being 'ruralized' by importing rural ways of life into the lower orders of urban society (Mangin, 1970, xiii–xxxix). This idea throws the question of the 'culture of cities' into clear relief. If 'ruralization' occurs in the lower social strata of the Third World city, extending, as McGee suggests, to even peasant modes of production (McGee, 1973; Isaac, 1974), what about the higher social strata? Are they being ruralized as well, do they evolve their own indigenous forms of urban culture, are they merely imitative of western forms of urban life, or is their cultural reality a more complex mixture of tradition, imitation, and innovativeness?

In the neo-colonial city, whose social structure reflects some form of dependent capitalism, it is possible to distinguish four social strata or classes: the elites, the middle classes, the working class, and the subproletariat. Beyond the city itself is the mass of the peasantry which exhibits a system of social stratification of rich and poor, landed and landless, with further distinctions based on the nature of the prevailing tenure system, the extent of involvement in the money economy, and the extent to which wages have replaced production for subsistence. If we begin with some such picture of urban society in its larger setting, it is possible to begin to say something useful about urban culture. The dominant urban elites, for example, tend for the most part to adopt life styles mimetic of western

38

models (Bugnicourt, 1973-4), while the predominantly white collar middle classes try to imitate as best they can the life styles of the urban elites without, in fact, being able to break through the social barriers to entry into the world of the elites. The working class, holding jobs in the corporate sector of the urban economy (Friedmann and Sullivan, 1974), are most likely to evolve their own culture, being fortified in this not only by their relatively stable employment but also by their virtual inability ever to rise to middle-class status within a single generation (Bonilla, 1964; Reyna, 1972; Peil, 1972).

If there is any class, then, that imports rural life styles and peasant-like modes of production to the city, it is the proto-proletariat which in many cities may account for between 25 and 40 per cent of the population. But even here, the evidence is divided. The frequency of rural ties in African cities, as reported by Weisner (1973) among others, suggests that rural social patterns are at first replicated in the city and change only gradually as a result of prolonged urban experience. But in Latin America Leeds and Leeds (1971) have presented extensive evidence from their work among the squatters of Rio de Janeiro and Lima that sharply contradicts what they disparagingly call the myth of urban rurality.

The city's ecology, in turn, reflects the complex social and cultural patterning of the city. Tribal, ethnic, and religious clustering is still the common practice in Africa and Middle Eastern cities (Hanna and Hanna, 1969a; Timms, 1971; Abu-Lughod, 1971), but class distinctions predominate in Latin America where the elites attempt to protect their own life styles by putting as much distance as possible between their own residences and the shanty-towns of the proletariat (Amato, 1970). In view of the massive influx of rural migrants into Third World cities, however, and the inability of the urban economy to absorb them into productive occupations (McGee, 1971a, chapter 3), one may well conclude that 'rurality' may eventually engulf the incipient cultural forms of dependent capitalism. Abu-Lughod's 'City Victorious' (1971) may yet turn out to be a pyrrhic victory.

The following four sections purport to review all that we have learned about urban life but also indicate the major gaps in our knowledge. The arrangement of topics follows the order in which a rural migrant to the city might experience them: urban morphology, social organization, the urban economy, and urban politics and social control.

1 Urban morphology and its determinants

Cities in the Third World are a morphological conundrum. Order exists, and even migrants newly arrived in the city soon learn to use the intricacies of its social and economic topography. They have to in order to survive. Yet the order is often unfamiliar to the western eye, and its high degree of complexity is often puzzling.

Research on the morphology of cities has been carried out almost exclusively by western scholars who, disdaining the cognitive maps of native populations, have relied on models drawn from studies in economic land use and social ecology.[10] Models of the first sort, based on classical price and rent theory, have been used to account for the spatial distribution of commercial and industrial activities within the city while ecological models have been used almost exclusively to study the residential choices of individual households.

a Land use studies: Constructing broad generalizations about Third World cities is always a hazardous business. Yet if a single fact stands out, it is that cross-cultural studies of urban land use have consistently reported the existence of a 'dual city'. These *colonial* cities, as McGee (1967) has called them, owe their dualistic structure to the intrusions of Western capitalism into forms of traditional culture. Existing side by side, and only weakly interrelated, both the 'modern' and traditional city display their own morphological patterns and residential behaviour (see the literature review by Ginsburg, 1965).

The traditional city (the *medina* of the Middle East) almost always displays some variant of the pre-colonial pattern. Breese's description of Delhi may convey a sense of what such a city is like (1966, 64).[11]

Generally, the Old City is a mile or less in diameter, though it may, as in Delhi, house a great majority of the population. Originally—and sometimes to the present, as in the case of Delhi—the Old City was surrounded by walls pierced by a few gates. Heavily residential in character, the Old City nevertheless shares its limited space with other uses. The house tax assessment registers of Delhi, for example, reveal that in Delhi's walled city 42 per cent of its houses are put to non-residential use, with 35 per cent having shops and 6 per cent industry godowns. . . . Gates and doorways open to private residences and courtyards, or to *katras*. The density of residence and its mixture of land uses is high, made more tolerable, perhaps, by the fact that residents may achieve some privacy from facing on internal courtyards, and not on the street. There is a considerable amount of segregation—some voluntary, some not—into small areal groupings, or into *mohallas* by caste, language group, geographical origin, religion (e.g., Moslems in the vicinity of major mosques), and income group. Except for mosque areas and temple yards, there is virtually no public open space; indeed, even the streets are inadequate for the volume of traffic and life they carry. Here, for the bulk of the

---

[10] On the concept of cognitive maps, see Downs and Stea (1973). A forthcoming study by Stea and Wood will for the first time present comparative data on cognitive urban maps for four cities in a developing economy (Mexico).

[11] For more detailed descriptions, see Abu-Lughod's life-style anatomy of Cairo (1971) and de Blij's complementary study of Mombasa land use (1968).

population is the core of the city. The foreigner, in an unfamiliar universe, finds it both hard to find his way, and hard to understand.

Much of the life in the traditional city takes place in the street. Indeed, many service activities which would occupy a specific piece of land in western cities are here conducted in a 'floating' space (McGee, 1974b). There are no clearly delineated 'functional' areas (focal points for religious worship and bazaars excepted), and no single use dominates an area. Western land use models are consequently worthless even to describe the typical patterns, much less to account for them. The 'involution' of space in the traditional city reminds one of the economic involution of employment which will be described more fully in section 3 below.

The picture is very different in the 'modern' city where one finds patterns similar to western capitalistic models, and where price, rent and zoning differentiate land uses into the standard functional areas. Always dominant is a central business district (CBD) where business, financial, and governmental uses generate high and even exorbitant land values, and where competition for space creates tendencies towards specialization along major arteries. Beyond the CBD, business ribbons often develop along major highways functioning as service areas as predicted by central place theory. A warehousing/wholesaling district may function as a distribution centre for imported manufactured goods and as a collecting point for raw materials destined for export. Residential areas are separated, often laid out in a standard grid of single-family dwellings, that are occupied by households of the urban elites as well as foreigners. When present, manufacturing is similarly segregated into industrial districts.

This co-existence of quite contradictory land use patterns within dual urban systems is unique to cities of newly industrializing countries. However, the precise morphological patterns differ from city to city. Two polar types may be distinguished according to the circumstances of their creation.

1 In areas of the Third World with a strong pre-industrial urban tradition, such as the Middle East, the 'modern' and traditional sectors are clearly delineated in space. The New Delhi-Delhi (old town) graft is an excellent example (Brush, 1962). Ibadan (Mabogunje, 1968), Cairo (Abu-Lughod, 1971, 182–93), Tunis (Brown, L. C., 1973, 29), and Chinese treaty ports (Ginsburg, 1965) are others.

2 The second type of dual city occurs where the city has been built under colonial auspices in areas devoid of any previous urban experience. Found generally in Africa (e.g., Lagos: Mabogunje, 1968), Southeast Asia (e.g., Kuala Lumpur: Sendut, 1965), and Latin America (e.g., Rio de Janeiro: Morris and Pyle, 1971), these cities were created to serve the needs of the colonial powers as ports, administrative centres,

and the like. In this type of city, the areas of traditional land use are less centralized; there is nothing equivalent to an 'old city'. Low-income, indigenous areas permeate the urban fabric, with some concentrations in the older parts of the city and on its fringes where a wide variety of so-called marginal areas may be distinguished (Delgado, 1971).

In concluding this discussion, it should be noted that these polar types are merely ideal constructs. Reality is always more complex. For example, Bombay and Calcutta which are both predominantly British creations display western functional areas in only modified form (Ginsburg, 1965, 316).

b Social ecological studies: Ecological research may be divided into those studies that seek to identify 'determinants' of socio-economic spatial patterns and those which focus attention on a description of the pattern itself. The former are strongly influenced by a model for the analysis of social areas which asserts that residential segregation can be fully accounted for by only three main variables: socio-economic status, family status (life cycle stage), and ethnic status (broadly encompassing religion, race, or linguistic affiliation). Isolated through studies of North American cities, these determinants of social areas have been tested in a Third World setting both deductively (McElrath, 1968; Abu-Lughod, 1969b) and inductively using the method of factorial ecology (Johnston, 1971a; Berry, 1971a). Their explanatory power has to some extent been validated by the research, but with the following important qualifications:[12]

1   Unlike American cities, family and socio-economic status are only weakly independent variables. Of the two, socio-economic status appears to be the more important determinant for segregating households, while family status is relatively less significant (McElrath, 1968; Abu-Lughod, 1969b; Schwirian and Smith, 1969; Pitts, 1971).
2   An additional determinant, migrant status, may be essential to include in studies of rapidly growing cities (McElrath, 1965; Clignet and Sween, 1969; Morris and Pyle, 1971). This functions by no means as an independent variable, however. Urban migrants vary considerably in socio-economic status and, on that basis, self-select (and create) very different kinds of urban neighbourhood (Flinn and Converse, 1970; Delgado, 1971; Brand, 1972).

[12] Not all urbanists are in agreement regarding the wisdom of comparative morphology. For example, the very act of a cross-cultural comparison of city forms has been criticized (Wheatley, 1963), and the validity of social area analysis and factorial methods has been questioned (Johnston, 1971b).

3   In cities surrounded by a poly-ethnic hinterland, as in Africa, ethnic
    status is likely to be a particularly powerful determinant of residential
    groupings (McElrath, 1968; Hanna and Hanna, 1971, chapter 6).
4   In India, caste and religion are the most powerful explanatory vari-
    ables (Berry and Spodek, 1971), with some internal segregation of
    caste neighbourhoods by socio-economic status (Bose, 1965).

These substantial departures from the classic western model may be
partly accounted for by the fact that, in contrast to advanced capitalist
society, newly industrializing countries, with their typical enclave economies, exhibit little socio-economic differentiation. The failure of socio-
economic status to separate from that of family, for example, reflects the
lesser degree of social differentiation in Third World cities. Thus the
three 'classical' determinants of western theory in the analysis of social
areas appear to be of only limited use in societies where spatial segregation
may be predominantly a uni-dimensional phenomenon (*e.g.*, in many
African cities, all but the elites are residentially segregated according to
the single factor of ethnicity). Some scholars have nevertheless argued
that the observed patterns of social segregation are merely 'transitional',
and that, once a society becomes 'fully industrialized', the classical
western pattern will once again assert itself (McElrath, 1968; Abu-
Lughod, 1969b). In Guatemala, for example, Roberts (1970) has found
that family status is beginning to effect household location. But these
predictions are clearly based on a capitalist model of development. A
socialist city might reveal a very different pattern.

Research into ecological patterns (as opposed to their determinants) has
generally involved a comparison with familiar North American models,
such as Burgess's concentric zone theory, Hoyt's emphasis on sectoral
patterns, and the multiple nucleation model. Applied to colonial cities,
these models often seem to 'fit'. For example, outward sectoral movements
by elites in four South American capitals (Amato, 1970) and Accra in
Ghana (Brand, 1972) have demonstrated the relevance of Hoyt's model
in those contexts, while Schnore (1965) claims to have found socio-
economic class distribution in two concentric zones for certain Latin
American cities, although the actual pattern turned out to be the exact
reverse of Burgess's original conception.

But these findings are exceptions. More commonly, significant differences are found that have been variously attributed to variables such as
level of industrialization (Gist, 1957) and technology of transportation.
Longitudinal data from Latin America permits an exposition of the
presumed relationship between industrialization and urban residential
patterns.

As a city industrializes, its traditional residential pattern begins to

43

disintegrate. The elite are the first to abandon the old city core and move to the suburbs, followed by the emerging middle sectors of the population. This leaves a declining downtown predominantly to the lower-income groups. As industrialization continues, and the middle sectors grow in number and variety, they begin to exhibit different social mobility aspirations and housing priorities (Turner, J. F. C., 1968b). Translating these aspirations and priorities into household location decisions, Johnston (1972) isolates two middle-sector subgroups—'upper class mimickers' and 'satisfied suburbanites'. The former are upwardly mobile and seek to occupy housing adjacent to the upper class in a kind of 'filtering' process. Satisfied suburbanites are less status conscious and consequently have less powerful urges to move up. Their housing priorities stress security by way of property ownership. Typically they move out to the city's edge where they occupy housing ranging from contractor-built suburban tracts to regularized squatter settlements.

This suburbanizing process is analogous to events in the United States and increasingly also in Western Europe, except that 'satisfied' urbanites have emerged much earlier under dependent capitalism in Latin America and have moved to suburbia at a much lower absolute level of living (Johnston, 1972, 115).

A central issue emerging from morphological analysis is the question of whether evolving urban forms in the Third World are converging on the model of the western industrial metropolis or whether some new synthesis will emerge. The bulk of the research cited above argues for convergence, claiming that continuing participation in the capitalist system will eventually transform the Third World city into the image of its western counterpart. But it is always dangerous to assume a unilinear evolutionary process. For variables which are implicitly held constant in studies of urban morphology in North America may well become determinants in a different cultural context. Examples of such variables might be:

1 *social structure*: the high ratio of ascribed to achieved statuses in Calcutta has created non-western residential groupings (Berry and Rees, 1969), as apartheid has done in South African cities such as Durban (Kuper, L., 1958).

2 *cultural values*: the existence of planned downtown shrines in Japan (Ginsburg, 1965) and the 'funeral quarters' in Cairo (Abu-Lughod, 1971, 193–7) suggest a divergent land use calculus, with sacred 'benefits' being counted alongside the more secular determinants.[13]

[13] The existence of 'sacred' values in land use decisions has also been demonstrated to exist in the United States. However, Walter Firey's early study of land use in central Boston (1947) has not been repeated elsewhere. Probably it deals with only a vestigial element in land use determination.

3 *history*: the rather inefficient morphology of some medium-sized cities in Japan can be explained by the historical inertia of their traditional forms as castle towns (Tanabe, 1959, 1970; Kobayashi, 1970).

It is undoubtedly true that the urban elites in Third World cities wish to imitate what they perceive to be the splendour of the West. The ruling class in Singapore dreams of New York, and its counterpart in Djakarta dreams of Singapore—a veritable hierarchy of dreams. But these dreams, whatever else their merits, may simply come to nothing under the impact of accelerated migration and the growing inability of the urban economy to absorb the incoming workers in productive occupations. The Third World city under dependent capitalism is predominantly a poor city, and the poor are growing in both absolute and relative numbers. The resulting ecology of poverty may be a very different one from the essentially middle-class cities of North America and Western Europe.

2 Social organization

In the preceding section, we saw how migrants to Third World cities encounter there an intricate, involuted ordering of spatial relationships. It is now our task to look at this pattern more closely and to review what we have learned about the nature of the city's social organization.

Every urbanite is at the same time a member of two contrasting social dimensions. The first is articulated *horizontally* and includes membership in kin and fictive kin groups, voluntary associations, and informal social networks. The second is articulated *vertically* into class structures of varying fluidity that are defined primarily by family, occupation, education, income, and life style. Speaking broadly, the new urban classes include a vast and ill-defined proto-proletariat (Gutkind, 1968b; McGee, 1974b), a much smaller blue-collar working class (Elkan, 1960; Lambert, 1963; Bonilla, 1964; Field, 1967; Peil, 1972), a vaguely characterized 'middle sector' (Johnson, 1958; Ratinoff, 1967), and a tiny but all-powerful urban elite composed of senior government officials and military officers, professionals, and financial and business tycoons (Smythe and Smythe, 1960; Lloyd, 1966; Lipset and Solari, 1967; Agulla, 1968; Goode, 1970a; Viloria, 1972). Urban social organization must be understood as resulting from the interpenetration of these two dimensions.

Until now by far the greatest attention has been devoted to the study of horizontal relationships among the proto-proletariat of cities. Early and rather simplistic beliefs that city life engenders feelings of *anomie* and, among the lower classes, social chaos have had to yield to massive, contradictory evidence. Although certain traditional functions of the family are being relinquished to secondary urban social institutions (Adams, B. N., 1969; Dore, 1971, 91–190), and the extended family is gradually being replaced by the typical nuclear arrangement (Goode, 1963; Fraenkel, 1964), social organization among the poor forms a rich quilt pattern of primary face-to-face relations.

Rather than disappearing, traditional kinship systems have been enlarged and redefined to accommodate the differing conditions of urban life. Rights and duties, for example, formerly associated with very specific types of kinsmen in rural areas, are associated in town with kin of all degrees (Mitchell, 1970). And, in the absence of a sufficient number of true kinsmen, kinship in the city is frequently extended to specific non-kin persons who are selected on the basis of 'second-best' criteria of affiliation, such as common ethnic or regional origin. These expedient relationships define a new category of *fictive* kin which impose on the parties involved codes of reciprocal rights and obligations similar to those which govern the conduct of true kinsmen in their relation to each other.

The persistent strength of kin and fictive kin ties has been reported hroughout the cities of the Third World. To mention only a few, there are descriptive accounts for Africa from Wilson and Mafeje (1963), Plotnikov (1967), Krapf-Askari (1969), Pons (1969), and Schwab (1970); for India from R. Turner (1962), Eames (1970), and Rowe (1973); for Latin America from O. Lewis (1959), Rogler (1967), Peattie (1968), and Butterworth (1970; for Southeast Asia from Bruner (1970), Rabushka (1971), and Hollnsteiner (1972); and for the Middle East from Abu-Lughod (1961), Gulick (1967), and Petersen (1971).

What appears to be a universal phenomenon always assumes particularistic forms in each locality and, in a more encompassing sense, in each specific cultural context. Nevertheless, certain common features have emerged that are worth noting. First, kin-based relations are especially strong and often all-pervasive among recent rural migrants to the city. Second, kin and fictive kin groups are highly localized in urban neighbourhoods at the street and block level. And third, interpersonal relations are so conducted that services (information, housing, food, and cash) as well as support (sociability and security) flow reciprocally among the members of localized groups.

Considering this evidence, it would be fair to say that the typical penurious urbanite, reluctantly received into the arms of an ever-expanding proto-proletariat at the bottom of the city's social order, finds his social relations dominated by kin and neighbourhood relations. Accordingly, he lives within a paradoxical environment. On the one hand, tightly knit social relations confined within a single neighbourhood help to soften the shock of his initial urban encounter; on the other hand, they may also inhibit his social and cultural assimilation into the wider world outside the neighbourhood 'enclave'.

Using Germani's (1967) distinction between social integration (i.e., participation in the larger urban society) and social adjustment (i.e., ability to perform an urban role without psychological dislocation), it becomes obvious that the neighbourhood enclave tends to accomplish mainly the latter while often preventing the former. The kin and fictive kin enclave facilitates the shift from a rural to an urban mode of living, but it tends to impede further upward mobility. Throughout the Third World, the proto-proletariat is encapsulated in a kind of ghetto, blocked from participation in wider social realms, only marginally absorbed by the urban economy, exploited by the elites, ignored by the middle strata, and viewed with deep suspicion, if not hostility, by the blue collar workers in industry and construction, anxious to defend their own and always precarious position.

The neighbourhood enclave has been the subject of the majority of the research on urban social organization. This is unfortunate, because the rather narrow scope of these studies has often led to misconceptions about the urban social system as a whole. The most common misconception involves the belief that lower-class social enclaves are self-contained 'urban villages' (Hollnsteiner, 1972, 30). Anthropologists, approaching these groups as if they were primitive isolates, are primarily responsible for this mistaken view. Neighbourhood enclaves have frequently been described as closed units without reference to their position in a wider urban, national, and even international system of relations of power. Quite clearly, however, these enclaves are subject to decisions at supra-local levels (Rollwagen, 1972; Epstein, 1972; Leeds, 1973), and ignoring their effects has resulted in myopic descriptions of proto-proletarian life styles of which Oscar Lewis' 'culture of poverty' (1966) is perhaps an extreme and certainly the best-known instance. In their rebuttals, scholars cognizant of underclass dependency, have tried to show how the 'deviant' behaviour of the underclass may justifiably be viewed as a rational response designed to cope with the consequences of their inferior social position (Eames and Goode, 1973).

Viewing the residents of neighbourhood enclaves as social isolates has also retarded understanding of their multi-facetted relationships with rural villages (see part III, section 4). But whether through circular migration (Weisner, 1973), monetary gifts (Shack, 1973, 270), or ritual (Buechler, 1970), the maintenance of rural-urban ties is a common feature of Third World urbanization, and we are just beginning to understand their significance for patterns of social organization (Lambert, 1962; Kuper, H., 1965; Nader, 1965; du Toit, 1968; Levine, 1973, Orellana, 1973).

Finally, urban anthropologists have been criticized for 'keeping their eyes turned downward and their palms turned upward' (Epstein, D. G., 1972). With only few exceptions (e.g., Vatuk, 1973), studies of neighbourhood enclaves have been exclusively concerned with urban poverty. So long as the focus of field research is on the neighbourhood, this bias may be understandable. But the kin-neighbour relation is much less significant for the middle strata and elites who command most of the city's resources and whose effective life space tends to be much more extensive than that of the lower class citizens. In fact, close kin-relations, whether spatially contiguous or not, tend to be regarded, especially by the middle sectors, as dysfunctional for their goals of social mobility and wealth accumulation (Marris, 1961; Mayer, 1961; Gutkind, 1965; Bryce-Laporte, 1970). For if honoured to the letter, reciprocal obligations among kin and fictive kin will lead to an informal income sharing that, in the final instance, is limited only by the needs for subsistence (Friedmann and Sullivan, 1974). It is therefore not surprising, as Johnson and Whitelaw have shown for Kenya (1974), that, as income rises, the marginal propensity for income sharing tends to decline.

Quite obviously, then, kin and fictive kin relationships confined to urban neighbourhoods do not exhaust the possible social relations in the city. Social groups based on neither kinship nor propinquity include functionally specialized groups such as clubs, civic organizations, and labour unions that recruit their members on the basis of voluntary choice, achievement, and membership in occupational categories. With increasing size of cities, the number and importance of these voluntary associations has grown phenomenally (Little, 1965; Doughty, 1969; Bogdan, 1969).

Among the urban poor, voluntary associations serve quite practical uses. There are co-operatives for making the most of limited resources (Abu-Lughod, 1961; Bruner, 1973; Rowe, 1973; Uzzell, 1974); special interest lobbies (Lynch, 1968; Cohen, A., 1969; Parkin, 1969; Hanna and Hanna, 1971, 170–80); groups whose purpose is to establish and reinforce a sense of shared identity (Little, 1965; Meillassoux, 1968; Germani, 1961; Doughty, 1970); and groups organized primarily for sociability and recreation (Goode, 1970b; Reina, 1973). In almost all these cases the dominant theme is mutual self-help.

Among the middle sectors and elites, voluntary associations reflect primarily a shared interest or status. Professional associations and trade unions in Africa, for example, cut across ethnic divisions (Schwab, 1965; Lloyd, 1969, 203–12; Hanna and Hanna, 1971, 128–31).[14] Like those in

[14] Among African elite and middle strata, traditional ethnic ties continue to compete with newly discovered class loyalties. Whenever it becomes acute, this conflict may impose a tremendous psychic burden on the individual who is attempting to resolve the conflict (Plotnicov, 1970).

Latin America, they come into being for the purpose of obtaining legislation favourable to the profession and for establishing credentials that restrict entry to the group. In Latin America western-style service clubs, such as the Rotary, predominate, along with clubs for sport, recreation, and other social functions, often organized along lines of national origin (Goode, 1970b). And in India members of the higher castes may band together for the preservation and promotion of regional languages and art (Eames, 1970).

Membership in a voluntary association not only locates a person (and his family) quite precisely on a specific rung of the social ranking system but also offers an important channel for upward mobility. Within the city of Paraná, Argentina, for example, a spatial hierarchy of social clubs, organized on the basis of *barrio, vecindad,* and city, roughly corresponds to working, middle, and upper-class membership. But if he should command the requisite amounts of wealth and education, an upwardly mobile individual may 'buy into' a higher-ranking social club and so achieve a sense of having risen in the social system (Reina, 1973, 138–70).

Club membership, however, does more than to confer social privilege and status. It also provides an opportunity for nurturing personal relationships that may smooth the path to achieving whatever one may need to further advance up the hierarchy of social power—a coveted job, a loan, a place within a private school for one's children, or a government licence.

The constellation of friends which every urbanite must cultivate and in which he may heavily invest in time and conviviality has recently become a major focus for urban research (Peattie, 1968; Whitten and Wolfe, 1973). Social network studies in both Latin America and Africa have found informal friendship networks to be the principal form of interpersonal relationship among upper social groups. In Africa, they have even been raised to the level of a quasi-ideology (La Fontaine, 1970) or culture (Jacobson, 1973) among the elite. Friends are used reciprocally as a source of help in a variety of situations, so that a friendship network may come in certain ways to resemble the fictive kin groups among the under class. But, with friendship and old-school-tie networks frequently stretching from one part of the country to another and across social classes as well, spatial contiguity is no longer important. One of the more common forms in which social networks are used is to mobilize support for local political campaigns (Epstein, A. L., 1961; Mitchell, 1969). From another point of view, closely-knit and overlapping networks of urban elites, such as those reported by Lloyd (1969) for Ibadan, Nigeria, exercise a pervasive, informal control over their entire social domain.

An especially significant aspect of social networks is that they frequently link up adjacent social strata. A key role here is played by 'gate keepers' and 'power brokers' who, situated in a lower stratum, have access to and enjoy the power that is derived from the one immediately above it (Adams, R. N., 1970). It is through power brokers and strata-spanning social networks that elites manipulate and, in turn, are manipulated by lower urban strata that need the protective benevolence of highly placed friends in order to survive in a highly restrictive social environment (Mayer, 1961; Gutkind, 1965; Vincent, 1971). It appears that such interlocking networks operate both within and between all major social strata but the lowest, though even here the proto-proletariat may be knotted into a far-flung system of personal relationships, particularly in multi-party political systems (Whitten, 1965; Leeds, 1964; 1973; Roberts, 1972). Social networks that extend across class boundaries may thus be regarded as one of the principal means for keeping the barriers sufficiently fluid to prevent a serious threat to the privileged positions of the rich and powerful who occupy the very top of the pyramid.

Power brokerage extends to even international relations. Foreign governments, corporations, and philanthropic organizations link into the dependent national economy through individuals who, by reasons of education, exposure, and training, have been sufficiently socialized to the dominant culture to react 'reasonably' and 'intelligently' to proposals for appropriate actions. These international 'power brokers' gain additional status and a certain domestic charisma from their international connections. They constitute a national super-elite that culturally as well as ideologically is co-opted by their foreign mentors. As certain Jews in Nazi Germany, they have become 'honorary Aryans'. It is primarily by exploiting local social networks into which these individuals are tied that the neo-imperialist European and North American powers are able to reduce their satellites to the status of a tributary economy and so ensure their continued underdevelopment and political pliability.

3   The urban economy

It would seem reasonable to suppose that economists are past masters in studying the economies of local areas. But for Third World cities this is not the case. In newly industrializing societies, studies of the urban economy are almost exclusively the work of anthropologists, sociologists, and geographers.

Still, it was economists who first identified the city as a problem locus. The source of their concern was the high levels of open unemployment but even more so the mushrooming of low-productivity employment in what was normally treated as the residual sector of the economy. Statistics were scattered and unreliable, especially on a local basis, and this was part of the problem. Nevertheless such data as could be brought together pointed fairly conclusively to the fact that modern corporate employment was a privilege attained by very few. Industrialization might raise GNP, but rising capital-intensiveness prevented the 'modern' sector from employing more than a small fraction of the available and constantly increasing work force in cities. This was contrary to European-American experience and contributed to a growing concern with political stability. Third World cities were different, and something needed to be done (Ridker, 1971; Kirsch, 1973).

The International Labour Organization was the first to ring the alarm. In a series of publications, the international dimensions of the problem were delineated, conceptual problems were clarified, projections were made, and policy questions were defined (Turnham and Jaeger, 1971; Galenson, 1971; Bairoch, 1973). Extensive efforts were also made to get governments to adopt explicit employment objectives alongside the usual one of growth in production. Technical missions were sent abroad to study the problems of urban unemployment in Colombia, Ceylon, and Kenya (see especially International Labour Office, 1972). But the immediate results were disappointing. For want of detailed micro-studies and models appropriate to them, policy recommendations proliferated but left the governments concerned confused.[15]

The absence of models of the urban economy was particularly serious, for without them observations tended to be made somewhat randomly. It was all the same, it seemed, whether one studied beggars (Fabrega, 1971), obscure occupations, such as Indian richshawallas (Gould, H. A., 1965), or native entrepreneurs (Marris and Somerset, 1972). In fact, quite a number of the studies focused on particular occupational types, for no other reason, one would suppose, than that such studies were traditional with anthropologists and sociologists and thus congenial to their methods. From a social and economic standpoint, the systematic study of informal income opportunities might well have been more profitable (Hart, 1973).

Such models as were proposed tended to be either structuralist and useful mainly for grand historical speculations about dependency, immiseration, and revolutionary potential (McGee, 1971a; Santos, 1971), or purely descriptive (Hart, 1973; Friedmann and Sullivan, 1974; McGee, 1974a). All the same and with the appropriate qualifications, these models served a useful purpose. Most importantly, they highlighted a sector of 'informal' employment that had heretofore remained obscure, even though it contained and helped support the majority of urban populations. Writing of Ghana, for instance, Hart (1973, 69) distinguishes not only between illegitimate and legitimate income opportunities in this

[15] Urban unemployment is not only a problem of dependent capitalism; it is also a major issue in socialist economies such as Cuba's (Mesa-Lago, 1972).

sector but, among the former, further differentiates *transfer activities*) petty theft, larceny, speculation and embezzlement, confidence tricksters, and gambling) from *services* (hustlers and spivs, receivers of stolen goods, usury and pawnbroking, drug-pushing, prostitution, poncing, smuggling, bribery, and protection rackets). Although only a small proportion of the labour force might actually be involved in these activities, the point is that even illegal occupations are capable of providing a modest living for those who have learned how to survive in them. A comprehensive concept of the urban labour market will thus have to allow for their existence.

The number of detailed analyses of the 'informal' sector is small, an incredible fact if one considers that from 60 to 80 per cent of the urban population makes its living in this sector. Monograph-length studies, such as Kilby's of the Nigerian bread industry and McGee's on Hongkong hawkers, are still a rarity (Kilby, 1965; McGee, 1974a). But data are beginning to accumulate, particularly with the renewed interest in small-scale industrial production and economically appropriate technologies (Hoselitz, 1968; Marsden, 1971; 1974; The Industrial Research Unit, 1972; Jackson, 1972; Callaway, 1973). Finally, there are a number of excellent studies of indigenous entrepreneurship in the 'informal' sector (Geertz, 1963; Katzin, 1964; Hazlehurst, 1966; Isaac, 1969; Hart, 1970; Marris and Somerset, 1972; Singer, 1972). It is here that the work of the urban anthropologist can perhaps make his greatest contribution. More than economics, it is the cultural influences which operate at this level that will determine the role of small-scale enterprise in the future of the Third World city.

Studies of entrepreneurship have their origin in the economic doctrine that development is essentially defined by the carrying out of new combinations, and that this innovative process of creating something new requires special attitudes we call entrepreneurial (Schumpeter, 1951, 66). 'The carrying out of new combinations is a special function, and the privilege of a type of people who are much less numerous than all those who have the 'objective' possibility for doing it. Therefore . . . entrepreneurs are a special type, and their behaviour is a special problem . . .' (pp. 81–2).

Schumpeter (1951, 82–94) was not of course thinking so much of the small businessman in the 'informal' sector as of the men who had carried out the industrial revolution in England and the European continent. This model of the rational, risk-taking entrepreneur may be contrasted with entrepreneurial behaviour in a different cultural setting (Cardoso, 1964; Lauterbach, 1966; Lipman, 1969; Singer, 1972). A study of industrial entrepreneurs in Chile, for instance, throws the differences into clear relief (Davis, S. M., 1972). According to Davis, Chilean industrialists behave in ways that contradict the Schumpeterian model on many points. The following propositions emerge from his research (287–92):

1 Survival replaces profit-making as the predominant orientation.
2 The focus of competition shifts from profit to power, and economic organizations become highly politicized.
3 The time-horizon of the manager is determined by changes in the political system more than by economic conditions of the market or of his enterprise.
4 Internal operations are believed to be less relevant to achieving organizational goals than is influence in the surrounding environment.
5 The board of directors of enterprise plays a very powerful role, whereas senior executives are of little consequence. Connection, not competence, determines performance.
6 Daily activities become radicalized, and normal conflicts become polarized. The result is a zero-sum approach to problem-solving.
7 The private enterprise system and managerial decisions made become sacred.

The practical implications of these statements are far-reaching. They suggest one of the reasons why dependent capitalism is incapable of generating cumulative and self-sustaining economic growth, and why the role of government, institutionalizing the entrepreneurial function, is likely to be considerably greater in the Chilean context than it has ever been in any European country or in the United States (compare Hartz, 1964).

4 Urban politics and social control

Francine Rabinovitz has argued that students of urban politics are never politically disengaged (Rabinovitz, 1973). Whether consciously or not, they are bound to be advocates for one or another political position. Ideas have consequences, and value neutrality does not exist.

This holds with more than usual force for those who study the politics of Third World cities. Urban politics has been very much an American enterprise, conducted within the framework of American political science. As such it embodies all the prejudices and internal politics of this academic discipline. For reasons that will become clear, three major topics have pre-empted the literature on Third World city politics: the politics of squatters, urban politics in general, and the administration of cities. At least in the first two of these, research methods have leaned heavily on quantitative and behavioural analysis with all that this implies: a neglect

53

of history, a failure to consider the initial distribution of power and the institutional arrangements that maintain it, a disinclination to judge political processes in terms of the results they produce, and a total unwillingness to engage in the construction of alternative social realities, if only as a basis for evaluating the existing one.

A good summary of the extant literature (excluding administration) will be found in Wayne Cornelius (1971; 1973). Many of the concepts which figure prominently in this literature, such as political socialization, political learning, and community, are practically devoid of meaning and, from a standpoint of social change, irrelevant. The one important idea to emerge, not startling in itself, is that the politics of urban life, so clearly part of the ongoing struggle to transform social reality, cannot be meaningfully isolated from the basic scaffolding of societal relations through which it is articulated and which ultimately determines its form and character.

Several reasons might be suggested why the politics of squatters became one of the central foci for research: squatters were not only there, but highly visible, and they engaged in political struggle for limited ends (Laquian, 1964; 1969; 1971; Goldrich, *et al.*, 1967–8; Roberts, 1968; Mangin, 1968; Powell, 1969; Ray, 1969; Goldrich, 1970). Also there existed widespread fear among local and foreign elites that squatments were 'hotbeds of radicalism' and 'powderkegs of revolution', and this ghost needed to be laid. The even more primitive belief, that squatter settlements were as socially disorganized as they were physically, was also entertained.

The research that was done tended to allay these fears (Nelson, 1969). It helped to tranquillize anxieties by concluding that squatters' aspirations were very much like those of other people—a job, security, a place in the sun, a decent and productive life, social esteem, and some of the material prerequisites of urban living. Because acting alone, an individual could not attain to all of these, he joined with others to achieve some limited good—a piece of land for himself, a house, a school. When the particular good that had moved him to action had been obtained, he lapsed again into his private sphere until some other need arose. And so he learned from experience: if you want to get something, you have to ask for it. And also: if you wish to be heard, you have to act collectively.

All this was expressed in language that served little purpose other than to veil the truth. The obscurantism of political science had become truly Byzantine.

Along the way, a few other things were found: squatments, like other neighbourhoods, clearly differed in their relative location and socioeconomic composition and consequently in their political behaviour (Cornelius, 1971, 114); and political parties competed with each other for the mobilization and support of squatter populations (Goldrich, 1970; Ross, 1972). But practical politicians have this knowledge in their finger-tips. They do not need to have it pointed out to them.

The politics of squatters is only a specialized topic in the study of urban politics (Alford, 1967). In this more general area, case studies also pre-dominate. African cities have been studied more thoroughly than any other (Epstein, A. L., 1958; Hanna and Hanna, 1969a; 1969b; Owusu, 1970; Baker, 1973; and Wolpe, 1974), but reports from other continents are beginning to accumulate (Weiner, 1967; Rosenthal, 1970; Bujra, 1971; Ebel, 1971; Lee, 1971; Lewis, J. W., 1971a; and Gamer, 1972).

Because politics is basically a way to get things done, it is a universal phenomenon that differs mainly, though not exclusively, in the importance of what, in the particular case, is at stake. Most Third World cities, how-ever, have little political autonomy and few responsibilities. The stakes are consequently low. This is true even for capital cities which, because they are large and important, tend to absorb a good part of the total work done in the national ministries. And where the allocation of resources is national, local politics is nationalized (Lee, 1971; Jones, 1973; Cohen, M. A., 1974). What happens in this case is that local territorial interests become subordinated to the segmental interests of functional groupings of the population, organized to influence national legislation that will benefit their members. Commercial, industrial, and professional interests are dominant, but labour unions may also have a significant voice.[16]

In Brazil and, indeed, in most Latin American countries, the power to get what you want is to a large extent mobilized through networks of personal contact among strategically placed age cohorts who are linked to each other through relations of reciprocal favours and obligations, friendship, and family (Leeds, 1964; 1973). The extent of spatial com-munity cohesion is thus extremely low. The bourgeoisie helps itself by activating the appropriate personal network described, while the lower classes—the working class and sub-proletariat—are shunted to the margins of the established society and, as much as possible, are left there to them-selves. It is in this context, then, that squatter politics must be viewed (Portes, 1972). Where the government is forced to intervene in pro of the squatters—the one group among the poor capable of some measure of self-organization in their own defence and thus a potential political threat—it does so merely to alleviate their condition, enough and no more

---

[16] In small countries which have a complete sample of industries but only one of a kind, the power of labour unions can be very substantial. A strike in a single industry may deprive the country of some essential product and create a national crisis. This is the reverse of the kind of power exercised by the industrialist who has a comparable stranglehold on the society. It is for this reason that the political control of labour unions in newly industrializing societies has become a major issue.

to keep them quiet and properly subservient (Perlman, 1971). For the time being these limited measures appear to be sufficient. As Portes (1970) has pointed out, the majority of squatters perceive their problem to be how to pass from the 'lower' city where they live to the 'upper' city of the elect who seem to control most everything that matters. In practically every instance the relevant authority for redressing social grievances is the national govenment. Local governments are almost universally weak and are controlled by the national police ministry (Ministry of Interior). In spite of this glaringly obvious fact, there exists considerable interest in studying how they are arranged and how they function.

Much of the motivation for this stems from a desire to promote the devolution of national power to local governmental units (Maddick, 1963; Sherwood, 1967). But there is little theory to guide the case studies in which the literature abounds (Ottenberg, 1962; Werlin, 1966; Walsh, 1968; Williams and Walsh, 1968; Walsh, 1969; Basalduo and Mereno, 1972; Robson and Regan, 1972; Richardson, I. L., 1973; Cannon, Fosler and Witherspoon, 1973). Most of these studies fail to make explicit the national context of culture, economic organization, and politics which is decisive for administrative studies. Public administration is a technical field, but even technicians may be in need of a supporting framework of shared understandings.

V   Policy and planning studies

Despite the wealth of micro-studies reviewed, the written materials on urbanization policy deal primarily with the distribution of productive activities and people across a nation's territory—the macro-aspects of urbanization. Variously referred to as a policy for settlement, migration, industrial location, urban growth, or regional development, with few substantive differences among them, we propose to call it a *spatial development policy*. With this we intend to convey the idea that the policy must relate urban to regional development, that core and periphery must be seen as constituting a single spatial system.

One reason for the relative neglect of local urban policies (as distinct from a national approach) is that the problems of large cities—poverty, tenement slums, squatter settlements, unemployment, and endemic shortages of public services—relate in one way or another to the 'informal' sector, to what Santos (1971, chapter 16) calls the *circuit inferieur*, Latin American sociologists refer to as *la masa marginal* (Nun, 1969), and the Latin American bourgeoisie quite simply calls *el pueblo*. This 'sector' of the urban population, impoverished but socially mobile (Muñoz and de Oliveira, 1973), has surfaced in large cities because of implicit spatial policies to concentrate investments at only one or two locations.

Ostensibly pursued for reasons of growth efficiency, these policies grow out of existing relations of power under dependent capitalism. They tend to encourage a rapid shift of population from rural to urban areas, often in excess of six per cent a year, in face of a total inability to absorb the massive increases in the urban labour force by any other means than 'involution'. Thus the problems afflicting *el pueblo* are incapable of being solved through local policy: they require a radically new approach to national development (Friedmann and Sullivan, 1973).[17]

Most discussions of spatial policy nevertheless accept the framework of dependent capitalism as given. Interestingly enough, the spatial policies of socialist countries, though clearly different in purpose and method, appear to be grounded in very much the same theoretical considerations (Dziewonski, Osborne, Korcelli, 1972; Latorre, 1972; Acosta and Hardoy, 1972, 1973; Luttrell, 1972–3; ODEPLAN, 1973; Farinas, 1973–4). We are therefore inclined to question Richard Willig's argument (1973, 180) that a change-over from capitalist to socialist planning requires a paradigm shift in theory as well as practice. Critical attacks on the theory of spatial policies planning that, such as Coraggio's (1972; 1973) and Harvey's (1973, 238), take their point of departure from a belief in the necessity of revolutionary transformation will have to be clearly distinguished from theories for social construction under an existing government. The logic of spatial development may be historically invariant. Differences in political orientation will merely change the ways in which this logic will be used.

In the following pages, we shall first review the literature on normative spatial policy, followed by a discussion of descriptive and evaluative studies.

1 Normative studies

Serious interest in spatial policy may be dated to publication of Lloyd Rodwin's important article on 'choosing regions for development' (Rodwin, 1963). There were earlier and partial formulations, particularly in the French literature (Boudeville, 1966), but Rodwin's was the first major theoretical statement in English. It was soon followed by

[17] Another reason is the lack of effective power at levels of local administration. In nearly all Third World countries, effective power is extremely centralized at the national level. There are some exceptions, such as Nigeria and India, where truly federative principles are being applied. But even in these countries, local authorities are rarely equipped to do more than the simplest kind of housekeeping job.

Friedmann's book on regional development policy in Venezuela (1966b) which went beyond Rodwin's formulation by elaborating a spatial systems framework for analysis. A number of other policy planners followed suit (van Raay, 1970–1; Hilhorst, 1971; Miller, 1971a; Hermansen, 1971; Logan, 1972; Fair, 1972). In line with Rodwin's and Friedmann's logic, they advocated a spatial policy for selective decentralization towards 'growth centres' in the periphery with a view to reducing major regional inequalities and strengthening the internal integration of the national space economy.

This deceptively simple formulation rests on a number of assumptions that go directly to the heart of spatial analysis:

1   that the economic development process is polarized in space and governed by the twin principles of 'initial advantage' and 'cumulative causation' (Darwent, 1969; Friedmann, 1972);
2   that highly polarized economic space, characterized by urban primacy, is undesirable from a national standpoint, and that a 'mature' system of cities tends to approximate the rule of log-normality (Berry, 1971b);
3   that large cities are generally more efficient from the standpoint of the national economy than small cities (Alonso, 1972; Richardson, 1973), but also that an economically efficient size of city can be obtained for population thresholds very much lower than those of existing major centres of urban concentration (Neutze, 1965; Spengler, 1967; Stanford Research Institute, 1969); and
4   that the spatial concentration of productive investments will generate not only self-sustaining, cumulative growth in the same location but also positive 'spread effects' from this location to surrounding areas of production (Mabogunje, 1971; Kuklinski, 1972; Boisier, 1972a; 1972b).

Nearly all of these assumptions have been challenged in the literature. The assumption, for example, that economic imbalances in space are generally undesirable and that policy should therefore encourage the selective decentralization of investments has been questioned by William Alonso (1968), Roland Artle (1971), and Koichi Mera (1973), among others. As these authors have suggested, large urban size is not inherently 'bad', and decentralization may lead to a decline in the overall rate of economic growth.

A completely different argument is advanced by Geisse and Coraggio (1972) writing on Chile. Their argument is worth repeating. Although it comes from the radical left, it arrives at much the same conclusion. They write (p. 58):

... the centralization-decentralization dichotomy tends to distract attention from the really important problem in Latin America. This is the necessity of permitting vigorous social restructuring and participation of all members of society for the benefits of economic growth, controlled and propelled by endogenous forces. With respect to the particular problem which concerns us here, and given agreement on directing the process of national development by evolutionary or revolutionary means, we attempt then to recognize that both the great city as well as the theoretical decentralized system may be instrumental in men's search for well-being. *Even though the process of centralization has been an instrument and an effect of the process of exploitation of the national hinterland by the national metropolis and of the latter by the international metropolis*, it is possible that in the future certain forms of deconcentration could be even more efficient instruments of internal and external exploitation of men by men. . . . And, just as it is admitted that the development of productive forces achieved by capitalism has been an improvement over previous forms of organization and should be exploited as a starting point for even better systems, so, too, can the great city be understood as a superior form of habitat required by man for his development. [Emphasis supplied.]

Also challenged has been the view that a 'mature' system of cities will tend to approximate the rank-size rule of urban population hierarchies. Although Berry's most recent researches are now widely regarded as conclusive (Berry, 1971b), the controversy about the meaning of urban primacy has raised some questions that are not completely answered in the Berry formulation (Davis. K., 1962; Mehta, 1964; Linsky, 1965; Sendut, 1966; Vapnarsky, 1969; El-Shakhs, 1972).

Finally, there is accumulating evidence that the 'spread effects' of urban economic growth, where they occur at all, are often of quite limited extent (see Part III, section 3). This may be true for a variety of reasons, including a form of agricultural organization which tends to isolate this sector from near-by urban markets, the high friction of distance prevailing in poor countries, substantial 'leakages' to areas outside the immediate region of production, and absense of significant 'backward linkages', particularly into the agricultural sector. Although some research findings exist in support of the 'spread' hypothesis (Nicholls, 1969; Gould, P. R., 1970), they can no longer be assumed axiomatically.

The challenge to a spatial policy of selective decentralization has been carried beyond the four basic assumptions listed above. E. A. J. Johnson (1970), for example, has strongly argued in favour of cities at the lower end of the urban hierarchy and advocates a market centre strategy in order to extend the presumed spread effects of urban economic growth into the rural areas. And in a recent article, Friedmann (1972–3) has shown that most forms of spatial integration rest on fundamental imbalances in economic and political relations, so that the objective of increased spatial integration need not always be regarded as desirable.

Many of these ambiguities are reflected in Friedmann's major review of issues in national urbanization policy (1973b, chapter 9) which is presented in the form of a dialogue partly to suggest the wobbly intellectual basis for what passes as the conventional wisdom of spatial planners.

In view of this situation, a major reassessment of spatial policies is under way. Rural development and problems of labour absorption in the urban economy are being emphasized as critical elements of this new doctrine (Salter, 1974; Ruttan, 1974; Marsden, 1974; McGee, 1974a; 1974b; Friedmann, 1974a).

Closely associated with this approach are policy studies relating to slums and squatter settlements. Here the focus shifts from the national space economy to the individual city and, within it, to the housing problems of the poor. By far the most influencial voice raised has been that of John Turner, a British architect-turned-planner, who set out to demonstrate that the squatting 'problem' might, in fact, contain the seeds of its own solution (1968a; 1968b).

More of a planner-advocate than Clinard whose excellent sociological studies (1966) of the same phenomenon are less well known, Turner became convinced that the problem of squatting can be traced to the lack of legal tenure rights for new arrivals to the city. Proceeding from this simple but fundamental assumption, Turner set out to elaborate a theory of squatments based on the relative 'need' of different social classes for identity, opportunity, and security (Turner and Fichter, 1972, chapter 7).

This represented somewhat of a *tour de force* in contrast to the more technicist writings of Charles Abrams, the leading housing planner in the preceding decade (1964), and it stimulated others to explore similar hypotheses (Mangin, 1967; Laquian, 1969; 1971; Juppenplatz, 1971; Rosser, 1972a). Although the removal of squatter settlements may continue unabated in a number of countries such as Brazil and South Korea, international housing experts and some national governments look increasingly for ways that squatters might be helped to improve their own housing conditions *in situ* (Leeds, 1974). Whether this policy is equally applicable to all countries remains in doubt, however (Fathy, 1973). And how it happens that the majority of large city dwellers is and remains poor is a question that is neither posed nor answered by Turner who basically remains a do-it-yourself advocate with an unbounded faith in the individual capacities of people to improve their condition in life through their own efforts. Turner fails to appreciate how this capacity may be constrained by an economic system in which the poor are basically regarded as a 'reserve army' of labour, and an aesthetic nuisance.

2 Descriptive and evaluative studies

Theoretical discussions of spatial policy were kept lively by controversies about big and little, cumulative causation and filtering down, efficiency and equity, spread and backwash effects, primacy and log-normality, and similar topics important to theorists. Meanwhile the practice of planning was quietly going on, as one government after the other began to engage in national planning for urban and regional development (Safier, 1970). By the mid-sixties the first reports on these experiences began to appear so that now, a decade later, a small library of publications is available to planners eager to expose their theories to the acid test of history. Unfortunately, none of these studies used explicit theories as a basis for evaluating practice, a fact which seriously reduces the scope of what may be learned from them.

In a class by itself is Lloyd Rodwin's collection of papers on Ciudad Guayana in Venezuela (Rodwin and Associates, 1969). This book provided detailed documentation on a major undertaking by the Venezuelan government to create a 'counter-pole' to the national metropolis of Caracas. The circumstances surrounding the Guayana project were rather special. The region had a rich base in natural resources, political stability was maintained, the government had money to finance the project, and the area to be developed was a nearly virgin space—the classical case of a resource frontier. Rodwin had acted as co-ordinator of the MIT-Harvard Joint Center of Urban Studies team that helped the Venezuelan government to plan for this new region; the book was his grand summing up.

In many ways the Guayana project may be called successful, if success is measured by the viability of the city that came into being. But the project also fell short of many dreams the planners held initially, partly because the city could not be dissociated from the larger national and international context of which it was a part. Then, too, the planners had to learn that even the extraordinary controls exercised by the Venezuelan Guayana Corporation did not provide for a perfectly controlled environment. Guayana never came to resemble the stereotypical planned city. Its growth was 'guided' but not 'planned'.

In interesting contrast to Ciudad Guayana is David Epstein's study of Brasilia (Epstein, 1973). Whereas Guayana is essentially an industrial city, Brasilia serves as the capital of the second largest nation in the Americas and is very much a planned city, conforming to a preconceived design. Less well known than Brasilia is Villa Bandeirante, a nearby worker's town left over from the period of intense construction. Today, its population rivals that of Oscar Niemeyer's monument to his own genius, and successive efforts at slum clearance have failed to wipe out this most

Brazilian of all cities, a spontaneous creation of the people themselves. Villa Bandeirante may be read as a perfect illustration of Turner's thesis.

Ciudad Guayana and Brasilia might both be called New Towns. They were, however, isolated instances in their respective countries. The most famous case in the Third World of a national policy for construction of New Towns is Israel. Two of the more interesting studies of the Israeli experience are by Shachar (1971) and Comay and Kirschenbaum (1973). As with Ciudad Guayana, the reading of the evidence is mixed. Although Israel proved that it could build New Towns, altogether too many of them failed to acquire a vibrant economic life of their own, and the economic costs failed to be reckoned.

Part of the problem was that the economics of New Town construction was made subordinate to ideology (Altman and Rosenbaum, 1973; compare also Stephenson, 1970). The idea was partly to occupy and settle the land, to serve defence, and to absorb the large contingents of new immigrants from abroad. Towards these ends, Israeli planners applied the principles of central place theory to the location of New Towns and the assignment of their economic functions. But the planners had underestimated the metropolitan 'pull' of Tel Aviv and Haifa which would compete for the attention of the new settlers. As a result a number of New Towns not only lost their 'function' to the larger cities, but a good part of their populations as well.[18]

Less flamboyant national policies for spatial development are reviewed in Lloyd Rodwin's monograph *Nations and Cities* (Rodwin, 1970). In addition to a recapitulation of the Guayana story, the book contains accounts of spatial policies planning in Great Britain, France, the United States, and Turkey. The experience of these countries is recounted in exhaustive, historical detail, but in the end the detail overwhelms assessment of the policies themselves. In any event the Turkish case, in which Rodwin himself had had a hand, may stand as one of the more promising endeavours to 'guide' the spatial development of an entire nation and to put into practice a policy of selective decentralization (see also Rivkin, 1965; Tekeli, 1973).

Two other works may be mentioned alongside Rodwin's comparative study: Walter Stöhr's systematic review of regional policies in Latin America (Stöhr, 1972; English edition in press at Mouton) and Ellen Bussey's parallel analysis of spatial policies in Mexico, Italy, and the Netherlands (Bussey, 1973). Both volumes, however, attempt only the most cursory evaluation of past policies; a definitive assessment does not emerge.

Mention should also be made of shorter case studies of national spatial policies in collections edited by Geisse and Hardoy (1972), Kuklinski and

---

[18] An interesting comparison to Israel's New Towns policy is Ved Prakash's book on New Towns policy in India (Prakash, 1969).

Petrella (1972), and Jacobson and Prakash (1971a), as well as in individually published articles by Jacobson and Prakash for India (1967), Stren for Africa (1972), Luttrell for Tanzania (1972–3) and Shah for India (1974).

Any concluding commentary on these studies must be sparse. A review of the empirical evidence suggests that the planners' promise has rarely been fulfilled in practice, that the instrumentalities available to them are often inadequate, that today's plans are frequently based on yesterday's theories, that unintended consequences may threaten to wipe out the modest gains achieved, that ideology may be more powerful a stimulus to action than economic reason, that the implicit policies pursued by governments may have more far reaching effects than the explicit policies of planners in guiding population and activities to their locations, and that, above all, politics is always in command.

VI Conclusion: a decision-framework for social reconstruction

The last ten years have seen a remarkable upsurge of interest in the comparative study of urbanization. In the present essay we have tried for a systematic and critical overview of the literature produced and are now ready to ask, what have we learned from it? And what conclusions shall we draw?

The principal conclusion is that the traditional disciplinary approaches to the study of urbanization have entered a period of diminishing marginal returns. Who needs yet another documentation of squatter politics, and to what purpose? And do we need yet further demonstrations of the cumulative advantages accruing to investors located in primate cities? What shall we do with endlessly repetitive surveys of migrant motivations? What mysteries do we expect to find? And do we really need to know for city after city what proportion of wages earned is sent back home to native villages only to discover that the marginal propensities for making such remittances will differ among cities?

If we were to sharpen the criticism implied, it would fall into two parts, methodological and substantive.

a Methodological: the traditional approaches of social science study, encapsulated within separate disciplines, fail to seek out the critical inter-connections among the phenomena of collectively adaptive behaviour in which they have an interest.[19] A *collective phenomenon*, such as rural to urban migration, *may be regarded as a particular form of a statistical frequency distribution*. Although it is a subject of considerable interest to specialists such as sociologists and demographers, each master of his own research tradition, migration flows are actually the result of other urbanizing forces, such as the spatial flows of controlling decisions, capital resources, and innovations (see Part II, section 4). If therefore an explanation of migration is desired, it is the behaviour of these other spatial processes and the reasons for them that must be analysed in the first instance. Demographers may argue that the study of power, for example, is not their special bailiwick, yet without reference to relations of power all they can do is to *describe* migration; they cannot hope to provide a satisfying explanation.

b Substantive: Work within the traditional disciplines is guided by a misplaced concern for the construction of predictive theory. Yet we have seen that the 'urban transition' is an historical process which, in one of its many dimensions, also involves the transformation of economic, social, and cultural space. Any theory which proposes to predict social behaviour is therefore likely to enjoy at best a very limited validity. What it will manage to explain is simply a particular form of *adaptively rational behaviour* which displays greater or lesser stability with respect to an historically given set of constraints. Even the best of social theories will thus be overtaken by events that change the nature of these constraints or be confounded by the discovery of certain forms of rational behaviour that are adaptive to different sets of externally limiting conditions. What appears to be adaptively rational behaviour in one context may be irrational in another.

We may test this proposition by a crucial experiment that involves projecting recent trends into the future and the question whether the resulting pattern seems either viable or just. If it is not—and we believe that the present trends in the urbanization of the Third World will produce neither a viable nor a just society—then what appears as adaptively rational behaviour now is, in fact, *substantially irrational*. And any theory which seeks to 'validate' this behaviour by proposing to explain it would be equally irrational.

Each of the major research areas we have reviewed at both the macro- and micro-levels in the study of urbanization focuses on particular instances of collectively adaptive behaviour. It is concerned with statistical aggregates of individual actions. But another way of looking at this out-

[19] For a different but trenchant methodological critique of comparative urbanization studies, see Soja (1973).

come is to say that regional associations of migrants, the structure of urban labour markets, squatter settlements, urban primacy, interregional conflicts, and so forth are in fact produced by socio-economic conditions that determine the shape of the relevant decision space for each of the phenomena observed.

A *decision space* may be defined as a set of salient constraints for choice within a given problem setting—for example, how to find enough to eat, how to get a roof over your head, how to gain the attention of the authorities, how to make a profitable investment, etc. The decision space simply circumscribes the available alternatives and specifies the probable costs and risks involved in choosing one or another of the perceived courses of action.

For every social problem, three elements may be said to determine adaptive behaviour:

1 an *objectively* given decision space
2 the distribution of individual or *subjective* decision spaces
3 the *objective determinants* of these spaces

The first element consists of the laws, the social and spatial distributions of relevant characteristics, and physical arrangements that exist in equal measure for everyone and so in principle constrain, and often are designed to constrain, all possible choices with respect to a given situation. The second is the objectively given decision space as it appears to and is evaluated by the potential actors. It emerges in accord with at least four main variables: the relevant information potentially available, the information actually selected and perceived to be of use, the meaning attributed to this information, and the actor's perception of the means available to him for carrying through with a potential course of action. The third and final element relates to the objective conditions that influence and partly determine the actor's selection and perceptions. The potentially available and relevant information, for example, will vary, among other things, with the size and type of settlement, its location of a transport and communication 'surface', and the contact networks that relate the settlement in question to all possible sources of relevant information. The actually selected information and its interpretation will tend to vary with culturally determined attitudes, values, and perceptions, prior experiences, and attained educational levels. And the perception of the available means will vary with existing levels of income and ability to absorb risk, social connections, and the degree to which the actor is politicized. All of these variables condition the choices of actors affected by them. The actual choice, of course, will ultimately hinge on the 'pay-offs' expected from alternative courses of action which each actor evaluates

65

in terms of a variable set of salient and often conflicting 'preference functions'. It is in this way, then, that the statistical frequency distributions of collectively adaptive behaviour are generated.[20]

The concept of decision space will be primarily useful in two ways: first, it will help to explain the frequency and forms of spatial distribution of a particular collective phenomemon, and second, it is the proper focus for attention in the design of public policies. These two uses are closely related, since a social science which focuses on the study of decision spaces, the objective conditions for individual choice, and the consequent forms of adaptive behaviour is likely to produce results that are directly useful for policy and planning. It is by redesigning these spaces and by restructuring the conditions for their evaluation that policies can hope to have a lasting influence on collective behaviour. In addition the concept of decision space forms a conceptual bridge between macro- and micro-studies of behaviour that constitute the two complementary poles of urbanization research. For it is the macro-level processes that constrain and help to shape the decision spaces of potential actors in individual cities.

Our review of literature suggests that the decision spaces relating to most of the phenomena of collective behaviour associated with urbanization—growing inequality, mimetic elitism, location of public services, primacy, urban unemployment, rural exploitation—are ultimately structured by the prevailing relations of dependency with respect to major core areas both inside and outside the society.[21] If this is so, then any policy that reduces this dependency will change the prevailing forms of collectively adaptive behaviour and thus to some extent also the processes of urbanization at both macro- and micro-levels. But if dependency in its various forms—economic, political, technological, and cultural—is not reduced, all spatial policies will merely counteract a set of structural conditions that continuously grinds out the very problems which the policy is intended to alleviate. Such policies are not only difficult to sustain, they are unlikely to produce more than marginally significant results. Because of certain feedback phenomena, countervailing policies may actually intensify the problem to which they are addressed, as when the creation of new urban jobs or the construction of a new highway accelerates migration to the city. To be successful in the

---

[20] Not all behaviour, individual or collective, need however be adaptive. There are important, if infrequent, cases of creative (individual) and innovative (collective) behaviour, the very behaviour, for example, that would result in a restructuring of decision spaces or a resetting of the objective conditions that determine, *inter alia*, individual choice and collective behaviour.

[21] The currently best elaboration of this statement is in a book that has just been received: Alejandro B. Rofman and Luis A. Romero, *Sistema socio-económico y estructura regional en la Argentina* (1973). See also part III, section I of this essay.

long run, it is therefore essential that policies achieve a *permanent restructuring* of the appropriate decision spaces.

To advocate a reduction of both internal and external dependency, however, is not enough, since it tells us only what to have less of and not of what to have more. What is additionally required, then, is a project for *social reconstruction* under conditions of reduced dependency. Such a project, conceived on the level of society as a whole, involves an act of 'innovative planning' (Friedmann, 1973c, chapter 3). In any substantially rational action of this sort, the people are the main protagonist. They learn new motivations, but they must also be offered entirely new choices. And so, the call for reconstruction requires a striking vision of a new society that will acquire its own reality through the praxis of a self-centred development. Studies of urbanization or, more properly now, of societal development, should thus be guided by an ideology which challenges us to make the world possible for the kind of life we care to live.

VII   References

Abrams, C. 1964: *Man's struggle for shelter in an urbanizing world.* Cambridge, Mass.: The MIT Press. (307 pp.)

Abu-Lughod, J. 1961: Migrant adjustment to city life: the Egyptian case. *American Journal of Sociology* 67, 22–32.

1969a: Varieties of urban experience: contrast, coexistence and coalescence in Cairo. In Lapidus, I., editor, 1969, 159–87.

1969b: Testing the theory of social area analysis: the ecology of Cairo, Egypt. *American Sociological Review* 34, 198–212.

1971: *Cairo: 1001 years of the city victorious.* Princeton: Princeton University Press. (284 pp.)

Acosta, M. and **Hardoy, J. E.** 1972: Urbanization policies in revolutionary Cuba. In Geisse, G. and Hardoy, J. E., editors, 1972, 167–78.

1973: La urbanización en Cuba. In Schteingart, M., editor, 1973, 340–72.

Adams, B. N. 1969: Kingship systems and adaption to modernization. *Studies in Comparative International Development* 4. (60 pp.)

Adams, R. McC. 1966: *The evolution of urban society.* London: Weidenfeld and Nicolson. (191 pp.)

1968: The natural history of urbanism. In The fitness of man's environment. *Smithsonian Annual* 2, 41–59.

1972: *The Mesopotamian social landscape: a view from the frontier.* Unpublished paper. (34 pp.)

Adams, R. McC. and **Nissen, H. J.** 1972: *The Uruk countryside*. Chicago: University of Chicago Press. (241 pp.)

Adams, R. N. 1970: Brokers and career mobility systems in the structure of complex societies. *Southwestern Journal of Anthropology* 26, 315–27.

Agulla, J. C. 1968: *Eclipse de una aristocrácia:* una investigación sobre los elites dirigentes de la ciudad de Córdoba. Edicions Libera. (156 pp.)

Alford, R. R. 1967: The comparative study of urban politics. In Schnore, L. F. and Fagin, H., editors, 1967, 263–304.

Alonso, W. 1958: Urban and regional imbalances in economic development. *Economic Development and Cultural Change* 17, 1–13.

1971: The location of industry in developing countries. In United Nations Industrial Development Organization, 1971: *Industrial Location and Regional Development*. New York: United Nations, 3–36.

1972: The question of city size and national policy. In Funck, R., editor, 1972.

Altman, E. A. and **Rosenbaum, B. R.** 1973: Principles of planning and Zionist ideology: the Israeli development town. *Journal of the American Institute of Planners* 39, 316–25.

Amato, P. W. 1970: Elitism and settlement patterns in the Latin American city. *Journal of the American Institute of Planners* 36, 96–105.

Amin, S. 1972: *Contemporary migration in West Africa*. Dakar: United Nations, African Institute for Economic Development and Planning. (77 pp.)

1973: *In praise of socialism*. Unpublished paper. (25 pp.)

Arriaga, E. E. 1968: Components of the city growth in selected Latin American countries. *Milbank Memorial Fund Quarterly* 46, Part I, 237–52.

Artle, R. 1971: Urbanization and economic growth in Venezuela. *Papers, Regional Science Association* 27, 63–94.

Association of Japanese Geographers, 1970: *Japanese cities: a geographical approach*. Special Publication 2. (264 pp.)

Bairoch, P. 1973: *Urban unemployment in developing countries*. Geneva: International Labour Organization. (99 pp.)

Baker, P. H. 1973: *Urbanization and political change. The politics of Lagos, 1917–1967*. Berkeley: University of California Press.

Balan, J. 1969: Migrant-native socioeconomic differences in Latin America: a structural analysis. *Latin American Research Review* 14, 3–29.

Balan, J., Browning, H. L. and **Jelin, E.** 1973: Men in developing society. Geographic and social mobility in Monterrey, Mexico. *Latin American Monographs* 30. Austin: University of Texas Press. (384 pp.)

Basaldua, R. O. and **Moreno, O.** 1972: The legal and institutional organization of metropolitan Rosario, Argentina. In Geisse, G. and Hardoy, J. E., editors, 1972, 189–96.

Bataillon, C. 1973: Papel y carácter de las ciudades pequeñas. In Piel, J. *et. al.*, 1973, 183–229.

Berry, B. J. L. 1966: *Essays on commodity flows and the spatial structure of the Indian economy.* University of Chicago, Department of Geography, Research Paper 111. (334 pp.)

— editor, 1971a: Comparative factorial ecology. *Economic Geography* (June Supplement). (367 pp.)

— 1971b: City size and economic development: conceptual synthesis and policy problems, with special reference to South and Southeast Asia. In Jacobson, L. and Prakash, V., editors, 1971, 111–56.

— 1972: Hierarchical diffusion: the basis of developmental filtering and spread in a system of growth centres. In Hansen, N. M., editor, 1972, 108–38.

Berry, B. J. L. and **Neils, E.** 1969: Location, size, and shape of cities as influenced by environmental factors: the urban environment writ large. In Perloff, H. S., editor, 1969, 257–304.

Berry, B. J. L. and **Rees, P. H.** 1969: The factorial ecology of Calcutta. *American Journal of Sociology* 75, 445–91.

Berry, B. J. L. and **Spodek, H.** 1071: Comparative ecologies of large Indian cities. In Berry, B. J. L., editor, 1971a, 266–85.

Beyer, G. H., editor, 1967: *The urban explosion in Latin America.* Ithaca: Cornell University Press. (360 pp.)

Biederman, J. 1974: *Enclave development: the case of multinational assembly industries on Mexico's northern border.* Department of City and Regional Planning, University of California at Berkeley: Master's thesis. (86 pp.)

Bloomberg, W. and **Schmandt, H.**, editors, 1968: *Power, poverty and urban policy.* Beverley Hills: Sage. (604 pp.)

Bogdan, R. 1969: Youth clubs in a West African city. In Meadows, P. and Mizruchi, E. H., editors, 1969, 223–41.

Boisier, S. 1972a: Industrialización, urbanización polarización: hacia un enfoque unificado. *Revista Latinoamericana des Estudios Urbano Regionales* 2, 35–62.

— 1972b: *Polos de desarrollo: hipótesis políticas. Estudio de Bolívia, Chile y Perú.* United Nations, Institute for Social Development Research. (172 pp.)

Bonilla, F. 1964: The urban worker. In Johnson, J. J., editor, 1964, 186–205.

Bonilla, F. and **Girling, R.**, editors, 1973: *Structures of dependency.* Stanford University, Institute of Political Studies. (262 pp.)

Bose, N. K. 1965: Calcutta: a premature metropolis. *Scientific American* 213, 90–102.

Boudeville, J.-R. 1966: *Problems of regional economic planning.* Edinburgh: Edinburgh University Press. (192 pp.)

Braidwood, R. J. and **Willey, G. R.,** editors, 1962: *Courses toward urban life. Archaeological considerations of some cultural alternates.* Chicago: Aldine. (371 pp.)

Brand, R. R. 1972: The spatial organization of residential areas in Accra, Ghana, with particular reference to aspects of modernization. *Economic Geography* 48, 284–98.

Brandt, H., Schubert, B., and **Gerken, E.** 1972: *The industrial town as factor of economic and social development: the example of Jinja, Uganda.* München: Weltforumverlag. (451 pp.)

Breese, G. 1966: *Urbanization in newly developing countries.* Englewood Cliffs, N.J.: Prentice Hall. (151 pp.)

editor, 1969: *The city in newly developing countries: readings on urbanism and urbanization.* Englewood Cliffs, N.J.: Prentice-Hall. (555 pp.)

Brown, L. A. 1974: Diffusion in a growth pole context: a comment. *Studies in the Diffusion of Innovation* 3. Department of Geography, The Ohio State University. (15 pp.)

Brown, L. A. and **Lentnek, B.** 1973: Innovation diffusion in a developing economy: a mesoscale view. *Economic Development and Cultural Change* 21, 274–92.

Brown, L. C., editor, 1973: *From Madina to metropolis: heritage and change in the Near Eastern city.* Princeton: The Darwin Press. (343 pp.)

Browning, H. L. and **Feindt, W.** 1969: Selectivity of migrants to a metropolis in a developing country: a Mexican case study. *Demography* 6, 347–57.

Bruner, E. M. 1970: Medan: the role of kinship in an Indonesian city. In Mangin, W., editor, 1970, 122–34.

1973: Kin and non-kin. In Southall, A., editor, 1973, 373–92.

Brunner, R. and **Brewer, G.,** editors, (in press): *Political development and change.* New York: Free Press.

Brush, J. E. 1962: The morphology of Indian cities. In Turner, R., editor, 1962, 57–70.

Bryce-Laporte, R. S. 1970: Urban relocation and family adaptation in Puerto Rico: a case study in urban anthropology. In Mangin, W., editor, 1970, 85–97.

Buechler, H. C. 1970: The ritual dimension of rural-urban networks: the fiesta system in the northern highlands of Bolivia. In Mangin, W., editor, 1970, 62–71.

Bugincourt, J. 1973–4: Interaction des catégories sociales et groupes sociaux dans les zones 'retardées' d'Afrique intertropicale. In Stuckey, B., editor, 1973-4, 49-82.

Bujra, A. S. 1971: *The politics of stratification: a study of political change in a south Arabian town.* London: Oxford University Press. (201 pp.)

Bussey, E. M. 1973: *The flight from rural poverty—how nations cope.* Lexington, Mass.: D. C. Heath. (132 pp.)

Butterworth, D. S. 1970: A study of the urbanization process among Mixtec migrants from Tilantoago in Mexico City. In Mangin, W., editor, 1970, 98-114.

Cadei, P. E. 1974: *A spatial approach to the study of power: a new dimension for political scientists.* University of California at Los Angeles, Department of Political Science. (47 pp. Mimeo.)

Caldwell, J. C. 1969: *African rural–urban migration: the movement to Ghana's towns.* New York: Columbia University Press. (257 pp.)

Callaway, A. 1973: *Nigerian enterprise and the employment of youth: study of 225 businesses in Ibadan.* NISER Monograph Series 2, Ibadan: Nigerian Institute of Social and Economic Research. (57 pp.)

Cameron, D. R., Hendricks, J. S., and **Hofferbert, R. I.** 1972: Urbanization, social structure, and mass politics: a comparison within five nations. *Comparative Political Studies,* 5, 259-90.

Cannon, M. W., Fosler, R. S., and **Witherspoon, R.** 1973: *Urban government for Valencia, Venezuela.* New York: Praeger. (152 pp.)

Cardoso, F. H. 1964: *Empressario industrial e desenvolvimento económico no Brasil.* São Paulo: Difusão Europeia do Livro. (196 pp.)

Chandler, T. and **Fox, G.** 1974: *3,000 years of urban growth.* New York: Academic Press. (460 pp.)

Chang, S.-D. 1963: The historical trend of Chinese urbanization. *Annals of the American Association of Geographers* 53, 109-43.

Chen, C.-S. 1973: Population growth and urbanization in China, 1953-1970. *The Geographical Review* 63, 55-72.

Childe, G. V. 1950: The urban revolution. *Town Planning Review* 21, 3-17.

1951: *Man makes himself.* New York: Mentor Books. (192 pp.)

Clinard, M. B. 1966: *Slums and community development: experiments in self-help.* New York: The Free Press. (395 pp.)

Clignet, R. and **Sween, J.** 1969: Accra and Abidjan: a comparative examination of the theory of increase in scale. *Urban Affairs Quarterly* 4, 297-324.

Cohen, A. 1969: *Custom and politics in urban Africa.* Berkeley: University of California Press. (252 pp.)

Cohen, M. A. 1974: *Urban policy and political conflict in Africa: a study of the Ivory Coast.* Chicago: University of Chicago Press.

Comay, Y. and **Kirschenbaum, A.** 1973: The Israeli new town: an experiment at population distribution. *Economic Development and Cultural Change* 22, 124–34.

Coraggio, J. L. 1972: Hacia una revisión de la teoría de los polos de desarrollo. *Revista Latinoamericana de Estudios Urbano Regionales* II, 25–40.

1973: Polarización, desarrollo e integración. *Revista Latinoamericana de Estudios Urbano Regionales* III, 121–34.

Cornelius, W. A., Jr. 1971: The political sociology of cityward migration in Latin America: toward empirical theory. In Rabinovitz, F. F. and Trueblood, F. M., editors, 1971, 95–150.

1973: *Political learning among the migrant poor: the impact of residential context.* A Sage Professional Paper. Comparative Politics Series 4. Beverley Hills: Sage. (88 pp.)

editor, 1974: *Latin American urban research* 3. Beverley Hills: Sage.

Cox, K., Reynolds, D., and **Rokkan, S.,** editors, 1974: *Locational approaches to power and conflict.* Beverley Hills: Sage.

Daland, R. T., editor, 1969: *Comparative urban research, the administration and politics of cities.* Beverley Hills: Sage. (361 pp.)

Darwent, D. F. 1969: Growth poles and growth centre in regional planning—a review. *Environment and Planning* I, 5–31.

Davis, K. 1962: *Las causas y efectos del fenómeno de primácia urban con referencia especial a America Latina.* Coyoacan, Mexico: Instituto de Investigaciones Sociales.

1969: *World urbanization 1950–1970.* Vol. I. *Basic data for cities, countries, and regions.* University of California. Institute of International Studies, Population Monograph Series 4. Berkeley: University of California. (318 pp.)

1972: *World urbanization 1950–1970.* Vol. II. *Analysis of trends, relationships, and development.* University of California, Institute of International Studies, Population Monograph Series 9. Berkeley: University of California. (319 pp.)

Davis, S. M. 1972: The politics of organizational underdevelopment in Chile. In Davis, S. M. and Goodman, L. W., editors, 1972, 31–4.

Davis, S. M. and **Goodman, L. W.,** editors, 1972: *Workers and managers in Latin America.* Lexington, Mass.: D. C. Heath. (308 pp.)

Delgado, C. 1971: Three proposals regarding accelerated urbanization problems in metropolitan areas: the Lima case. In Miller and Gakenheimer, editors, 1971, 269–310.

Deutsch, K. 1953: The growth of nations: some recurrent patterns of political and social integration. *World Politics* 5, 168–95.

de Blij, H. J. 1968: *Mombasa, an African city.* Evanston: Northwestern University Press. (168 pp.)

Diaz, M. N. 1966: *Tonala: conservatism, responsibility, and authority in a Mexican town.* Berkeley: University of California Press.

Dore, R. P. 1971: *City life in Japan.* 3rd edition. Berkeley: University of California Press. (472 pp.)

Doughty, P. 1969: La cultura del regionalismo en la vida urbana de Lima, Perú. *América Indígena* 29, 949–98.

1970: Behind the back of the city: 'provincial' life in Lima, Peru. In Mangin, W., editor, 1970, 30–46.

Downs, R. M. and **Stea, D.**, editors, 1973: *Image and environment: cognitive mapping and spatial behavior.* London: Edward Arnold; Chicago: Aldine. (439 pp.)

Duchacek, I. 1970: *Comparative federalism: the territorial dimension of politics.* New York: Holt, Rinehard and Winston. (370 pp.)

Dunn, E. S. 1971: *Economic and social development: a process of social learning.* Baltimore: The Johns Hopkins Press. (327 pp.)

du Toit, B. M. 1968: Cultural continuity and African urbanization. In Eddy, E., editor, 1968, 58–74.

Dwyer, D. J., editor, 1972: *The city as a centre of change in Asia.* Hong Kong: Hong Kong University Press. (287 pp.)

Dziewonski, K., Osborne, R. H., and **Korcelli, P.,** editors, 1972: *Geographia Polonica* 24. Special issue on Geographical Aspects of Rural–Urban Interaction. (254 pp.)

Eames, E. 1970: Corporate groups and Indian urbanization. *Anthropological Quarterly* 43, 168–86.

Eames, E. and **Goode, J. G.** 1973: *Urban poverty in a cross-cultural context.* New York: Free Press.

Ebel, R. H. 1971: The decision-making process in San Salvador. In Rabinovitz, F. F. and Trueblood, F., editors, 1971, 189–216.

Economic Commission for Latin America, 1974: Income distribution in selected major cities of Latin America and in their respective countries. *Economic Bulletin for Latin America* 18, 13–45.

Eddy, E., editor, 1968: *Urban anthropology: research perspectives and strategies.* Athens, Georgia: University of Georgia Press. (100 pp.)

El-Badry, N. A. 1965: Trends in the components of population growth in the Arab countries of the Middle East: a survey of present information. *Demography* 2, 140–86.

Elkan, W. 1960: *Migrants and proletarians: urban labour in the economic development of Uganda.* London: Oxford University Press. (149 pp.)

1967: Circular migration and the growth of towns in East Africa. *International Labour Review* 96, 581–89.

Ellefson, R. A. 1962: City-hinterland relationships in India. In Turner, R., editor, 1962, 94–116.

El-Shakhs, S. 1972: Development, primacy, and system of cities. *The Journal of Developing Areas* 7, 11–36.

Epstein, A. L. 1958: *Politics in the urban African community*. Manchester: Manchester University Press. (254 pp.)

1961: The network and urban social organization. *Rhodes-Livingstone Journal* 29, 129–62.

1967: Urbanization and social change in Africa. *Current Anthropology* 8, 275–96.

Epstein, D. G. 1972: The genesis and function of squatter settlements in Brasilia. In Weaver, T. and White, D., editors, 1972, 51–8.

1973: *Brasilia—plan and reality: a study of planned and spontaneous settlement.* Berkeley: University of California Press. (206 pp.)

Fabrega, H. 1971: Begging in a southeastern Mexican city. *Human Organization* 30, 277–87.

Fair, T. J. D. 1972: *The metropolitan imperative.* Inaugural lecture. Johannesburg: Witwatersrand University Press. (24 pp.)

Farinas, R. R. 1973–74: El papel de la planificación en la economía nacional. *Revista Interamericana de Planificación* 28–9, 102–15.

Fathy, H. 1973: *Architecture for the poor.* Chicago: Chicago University Press. (256 pp.)

Feindt, W. and **Browning, H. L.** 1972: Return migration: its significance in an industrial metropolis and on agricultural towns in Mexico. *International Migration Review* 6, 158–65.

Field, A. J. 1967: *Urbanization and work in modernizing societies.* Detroit: Glengary Press. (209 pp.)

editor, 1971: *City and country in the Third World: issues in the modernization of Latin America.* Cambridge, Mass.: Schenkman. (303 pp.)

Firey, W. 1947: *Land use in central Boston.* Cambridge, Mass.: Harvard University Press. (367 pp.)

Flinn, W. L. 1966: Rural to urban migration: a Colombian case. University of Wisconsin Land Tenure Center, Reprint 19. (42 pp.)

Flinn, W. L. and **Converse, J. W.** 1970: Eight assumptions concerning rural–urban migration to Colombia: a three shanty town test. *Land Economics* 46, 456–66.

Fraenkel, M. 1964: *Tribe and class in Monrovia.* London: Oxford University Press. (244 pp.)

Frank, A. G. 1967: *Capitalism and underdevelopment in Latin America: historical studies of Chile and Brazil.* New York: Monthly Review Press. (298 pp.)

Friedmann, J. 1961: Cities in social transformation. *Comparative Studies in Society and History* 4, 86–103.

1966a: Two concepts of urbanization. *Urban Affairs Quarterly* 1, 78–84.

1966b: *Regional development policy: a case study of Venezuela.* Cambridge, Mass.: The MIT Press. (279 pp.)

1971: A theory of urbanization: rejoinder to Richard Morse. In Miller, J. and Gakenheimer R., editors, 1971, 201–208.

1972: A general theory of polarized development. In Hansen, editor, 1972, 82–107.

1972–73: The spatial organization of power and the development of urban systems. *Development and Change* 4, 12–50.

1973a: General theory in the study of urbanization. In Wulff, R., editor, 1973b, 144–50.

1973b: *Urbanization, planning, and national development.* Beverley Hills: Sage. (351 pp.)

1973c: *Retracking America: a theory of transactive planning.* New York: Doubleday/Anchor. (289 pp.)

1974a: *An approach to policies planning for spatial development.* Comparative Urbanization Studies. School of Architecture and Urban Planning, University of California, Los Angeles. (26 pp.)

editor, 1974b: *New concepts and technologies in Third World urbanization.* Comparative Urbanization Studies. School of Architecture and Urban Planning, University of California, Los Angeles. (231 pp.)

Friedmann, J., McGlynn, E., Stuckey, B. and **Wu, C.** 1971: Urbanisation et développement national: une étude comparative. *Revue Tiers-Monde* 12, 13–44.

Friedmann, J. and **Miller, J.** 1965: The urban field. *Journal of the American Institute of Planners* 31, 312–19.

Friedmann, J. and **Sullivan, F.** 1974: Labor absorption in the urban economy: the case of the developing countries. *Economic Development and Cultural Change* 22, 385–413.

Funck, R., editor, 1972: *Recent developments in regional science.* London: Pion Ltd.

Galeson, W., editor, 1971: *Essays on employment.* Geneva: International Labour Office. (320 pp.)

Gamer, R. E. 1972: *The politics of urban development in Singapore.* Ithaca: Cornell University Press. (263 pp.)

Geertz, C. 1963: *Peddlers and princes—a study of two Indonesian towns.* Chicago: University of Chicago Press. (162 pp.)

Geisse, G. and **Coraggio, J. L.** 1972: Metropolitan areas and national development. In Geisse, G. and Hardoy, J., editors, 1972, 45–60.

Geisse, G. and **Hardoy, J. E.,** editors, 1972: *Regional and urban development policies: a Latin American perspective.* Latin American Urban Research 2. Beverley Hills: Sage. (298 pp.)

Germani, G. 1961: Inquiry into the effects of urbanization in a working-class sector of greater Buenos Aires. In Hauser, P., editor, 1961, 206–33.

1967: The concept of social integration. In Beyer, G., editor, 1967, 175–88.

Ginsburg, N. S. 1965: Urban geography and 'non-western' areas. In Hauser, P. and Schnore, L. F., editors, 1965, 311–46.

Gist, N. P. 1957: The ecology of Bangalore, India: an east-west comparison. *Social Forces* 35, 356–65.

Goldrich, D. 1970: Political organization and the politicization of the Poblador. *Comparative Political Studies* 3, 176–202.

Goldrich, D., Pratt, R. B., Schuller, C. R. 1967–8: The political integration of lower-class urban settlements in Chile and Peru. *Studies in International Comparative Development* 3, 1–22.

Goode, J. 1963: *World revolution and family patterns.* New York: Free Press of Glencoe.

1970a: The response of a traditional elite to modernization: lawyers in Colombia. *Human Organization* 20, 70–80.

1970b: Latin American urbanism and corporate groups. *Anthropological Quarterly* 43, 146–67.

Goodman, A. 1971: The political implications of urban development in southeast Asia: the 'fragment hypothesis.' *Economic Development and Cultural Change* 20, 117–30.

1973: *The political consequences of urban growth policies in southeast Asia.* Unpublished MS, Annual Meeting of the Association for Asian Studies, Chicago.

Gould, H. A. 1965: Lucknow Richshawallas: the social organization of an occupational category. *International Journal of Comparative Sociology* 6, 24–47.

Gould, P. R. 1970: Tanzania 1920–63: the spatial impress of the modernization process. *World Politics* 22, 149–70.

Gould, P. and Ola, D. 1970: The perception of residential desirability in the western region of Nigeria. *Environment and Planning* 2, 73–88.

Green, E. L. 1973: Locational analysis of pre-historical Maya sites in northern British Honduras. *American Antiquity* 38, 279–93.

Greer, S., McElrath, D., Minar, D., and Orleans, P. 1968: *The new urbanization.* New York: St. Martin's Press. (377 pp.)

Gulick, J. 1967: *Tripoli: a modern Arab city.* Cambridge, Mass.: Harvard University Press. (253 pp.)

Gutkind, P. C. W. 1965: African urbanism, mobility, and the social network. *International Journal of Sociology* 6, 48–60.

1968: The poor in urban Africa: a prologue to modernization, conflict and the unfinished revolution. In Bloomberg, W. and Schmandt, H., editors, 1968, 355–96.

Guyot, J. F. 1969: Creeping urbanism and political development. In Daland, R. T., editor, 1969, chapter 4.

Hägerstrand, T. and Kuklinski, A. R., editors, 1971: *Information* *systems for regional development: a seminar.* Lund Studies in Geography, Series B, Human Geography 37, Lund: C. W. K. Gleerup. (266 pp.)

Hance, W. A. 1970: *Population, migration, and urbanization in Africa.* New York: Columbia University Press. (450 pp.)

Hanna, W. J. and **Hanna, J. L.** 1969a: Polyethnicity and political integration in Umuahia and Mbala. In Daland, R. T., editor, 1969.

1969b: Influence and influentials in two urban-centred African communities. *Comparative Politics* 2, 17–40.

1971: *Urban dynamics in black Africa.* Chicago: Aldine-Atherton. (390 pp.)

Hansen, N. M., editor, 1972: *Growth centers in regional economic development* New York: The Free Press. (298 pp.)

Harris, J. and **Weiner, M.,** editors, 1973: *Cityward migration in developing countries.* Cambridge, Mass.: The MIT Press.

Harris, W. D. 1971: *The growth of Latin American cities.* Athens, Ohio: Ohio University Press. (314 pp.)

Hart, K. 1970: Small scale entrepreneurs in Ghana and development planning. *Journal of Development Studies* 6, 104–20.

1973: Informal income opportunities and urban unemployment in Ghana. *Journal of Modern African Studies* 11, 61–90.

Hartz, L. 1964: *The founding of new societies: studies in the history of the United States, Latin America, South Africa, Canada, and Australia.* New York: Harcourt, Brace, Jovanovich (336 pp.)

Harvey, D. 1973: *Social justice and the city.* London: Edward Arnold; Baltimore: Johns Hopkins University Press. (336 pp.)

Harvey, M. and **Greenberg, P.** 1972: Development dichotomies, growth poles and diffusion processes in Sierra Leone. *African Urban Notes* 6, 117–36.

Hauser, P., editor, 1961: *Urbanization in Latin America.* New York: International Documents Service. (331 pp.)

Hauser, P. and **Schnore, L. F.,** editors, 1965: *The study of urbanization.* New York: John Wiley and Sons. (554 pp.)

Hazlehurst, L. W. 1966: *Entrepreneurship and the merchant castes in a Punjabi city.* Durham, N. C.: Duke University Press. (151 pp.)

Heisler, H. 1974: *Urbanization and the government of migration: the interrelation of urban and rural life in Zambia.* New York: St Martin's Press. (282 pp.)

Hermansen, T. 1971: *Spatial organization and economic development. The scope and task of spatial planning.* University of Mysore, Institute of Development Studies. (86 pp.)

1972: Development poles and related theories: a synoptic view. In Hansen, editor, 1972, 160–203.

Herrick, B. 1965: *Urban migration and economic development in Chile.* Cambridge, Mass.: The MIT Press. (126 pp.)

Herskovits, M. and **Harwitz, M.,** editors, 1964: *Economic transition in Africa.* Evanston, Ill.: Northwestern University Press. (444 pp.)

Hilhorst, J. G. M. 1971: *Regional planning: a systems approach.* Rotterdam: Rotterdam University Press. (151 pp.)

Hollnsteiner, M. R. 1972: Becoming an urbanite: the neighbourhood as a learning environment. In Dwyer, D. J., editor, 1972, 29–40.

Honigmann, J. J., editor, 1973: *Handbook of social and cultural anthropology.* Chicago: Rand McNally. (1295 pp.)

Horwitz, I. L. 1967: Electoral politics, urbanization, and social development. In Beyer, G. H., editor, 1967, 215–53.

Hoselitz, B. F. 1960: *Sociological aspects of economic growth.* Glencoe, Ill.: Free Press. (250 pp.)

editor, 1968: *The role of small industry in the process of economic growth.* The Hague: Mouton. (218 pp.)

International Labour Office 1972: *Employment, incomes and equality. A strategy for increasing productive employment in Kenya.* Geneva: International Labour Office. (600 pp.)

Isaac, B. L. 1969: Kinship obligations and entrepreneurship: conflicting or complementary. *Sierra Leone Studies* 25, 24–29.

(in press): Peasants in cities: ingenious paradox or conceptual muddle. *Human Organization.*

Issawi, C. 1969: Economic change and urbanization in the Middle East. In Lapidus, I. M., editor, 1969, 102–21.

Jackson, S. 1972: *Economically appropriate technologies for developing countries: a survey.* Washington, D.C.: Overseas Development Council. (38 pp.)

Jacobs, J. 1969: *The economy of cities.* New York: Random House. (268 pp.)

Jacobson, D. 1973: *Itinerant townsmen: friendship and social order in urban Uganda.* Menlo Park, CA: Cummings. (150 pp.)

Jacobson, L. and **Prakash, V.** 1967: Urbanization and regional planning in India. *Urban Affairs Quarterly* 2, 36–65.

editors, 1971a: *Urbanization and national development.* South and Southeast Asian urban affairs annuals I. Beverley Hills: Sage. (320 pp.)

1971b: Urbanization and urban development: proposals for an integrated policy base. In Jacobson and Prakash, editors, 1971, chapter 1.

Johnson, E. A. J. 1970: *The organization of space in developing countries.* Cambridge, Mass.: Harvard University Press. (452 pp.)

Johnson, G. A. 1972: *A test of the utility of central place theory on archaeology.* New York: MSS Modular Publications. (17 pp.)

Johnson, G. E. and **Whitelaw, W. E.** 1974: Urban–rural income transfers in Kenya: an estimated remittances function. *Economic Development and Cultural Change* 22, 473–79.

Johnson, J. J. 1958: *Political change in Latin America: the emergence of the middle sectors.* Stanford: Stanford University Press. (272 pp.)

1964: *Continuity and change in Latin America.* Stanford: Stanford University Press. (282 pp.)

Johnston, R. J. 1971a: *Urban residential patterns.* London: Bell. (383 pp.)

1971b: Some limitations of factorial ecologies and social area analysis. In Berry, B. J. L., editor, 1971, 314–23.

1972: Towards a general model of intra-urban residential patterns: some cross-cultural observations. *Progress in Geography* 4, 83–124.

Jones, R. W. 1973: *Urban politics in India: area, power, and policy in a penetrated system.*

Juppenplatz, M. 1971: *Cities in transformation: the urban squatter problem in the developing world.* Queensland, Australia: University of Queensland Press. (257 pp.)

Karpat, K. 1971: *The background of Ottoman concept of city and urbanity.* Unpublished paper.

Katzin, M. 1964: The role of the small entrepreneur. In Herskovits, M. and Harwitz, M., editors, 1964, 179–98.

Kilby, P. 1965: *African enterprise: the Nigerian bread industry.* Hoover Institute Studies 8, Stanford: Stanford University. (112 pp.)

Kirsch, H. 1973: Employment and the utilization of human resources in Latin America. *Economic Bulletin for Latin America* 18, 95–125.

Kobayashi, H. 1970: The modernization of Kyoto—from the morphological point of view. In *Annals of the Association of Japanese Geographers* (1970), 23–30.

Kraeling, C. H. and **Adams, R. M.,** editors, 1960: *City invincible. A symposium on urbanization and cultural development in the ancient Near East.* Chicago: The University of Chicago Press. (447 pp.)

Krapf-Askari, E. 1969: *Yoruba towns and cities: an enquiry into the nature of urban social phenomena.* London: Clarendon. (195 pp.)

Kuklinski, A., editor, 1972: *Growth poles and growth centres in regional planning.* The Hague: Mouton. (306 pp.)

Kuklinski, A. and **Petrella, R.,** editors, 1972: *Growth poles and regional policies: a seminar.* The Hague: Mouton.

Kuper, H., editor, 1965: *Urbanization and migration in West Africa.* Berkeley: University of California Press. (227 pp.)

Kuper, L. et al. 1958: *Durban: a study in racial ecology.* New York: Columbia University Press. (254 pp.)

La Fontaine, J. S. 1970: *City politics: a study of Leopoldville, 1962–3.* London: Cambridge University Press. (247 pp.)

Lambert, R. D. 1962: The impact of urban society on village life. In Turner, R., editor, 1962, 117–41.

Lambert, R. D. 1963: *Workers, factories, and social change in India*. Princeton: Princeton University Press. (247 pp.)

Lampl, P. 1968: *Cities and planning in the ancient Near East*. New York: George Braziller. (128 pp.)

Lapidus, I. 1967: *Muslim cities in the later middle ages*. Cambridge, Mass.: Harvard University Press. (307 pp.)

editor, 1969: *Middle eastern cities*. Berkeley: University of California Press. (206 pp.)

Laquian, A. A. 1964: Isla de Kokomo: politics among urban slum dwellers. *Philippine Journal of Public Administration* 8, 112–22.

1969: *Slums are for people*. Manila: College of Public Administration. (245 pp.)

1971: Slums and squatters in South and Southeast Asia. In Jacobson, L. and Prakash, V., editors, 1971, 183–204.

Lasuén, J. R. 1971: Multi-regional economic development: an open-system approach. In Hägerstrand, T. and Kuklinski, A. R., editors, 1971, 169–211.

Latorre, H. 1972: La planificación regional en el Gobierno Popular. *Revista Interamericana de Planificación* 6, 60–8.

Lauterbach, A. 1966: *Enterprise in Latin America: business attitudes in a developing economy*. Ithaca: Cornell University Press. (207 pp.)

Lee, E. S. 1966: A theory of migration. *Demography* 3, 47–57.

Lee, C. J. 1971: Urban political competition in a developing nation: the case of Korea. *Comparative Political Studies* 4, 107–15.

Leeds, A. 1964: Brazilian careers and social structure: an evolutionary model and case history. *American Anthropologist* 66, 1321–47.

1973: Locality power in relation to supralocal power institutions. In Southall, A., editor, 1973, 15–42.

1974: Political, economic and social effects of producer and consumer orientations toward housing in Brazil and Peru: a systems analysis. In Cornelius, W., 1974, 181–215.

Leeds, A. and **Leeds, E.** 1971: Brazil and the myth of urban rurality: urban experience, work and values in the 'squatments' of Rio de Janeiro and Lima. In Field, A. J., editor, 1971, 229–72.

Lefèbvre, H. 1972: *La pensée Marxiste et la ville*. Paris: Casterman. (155 pp.)

Lerner, D. 1958: *The passing of traditional society: modernizing the Middle East*. Chicago: University of Chicago Press. (466 pp.)

Levine, N. 1973: Old culture—new culture: a study of migrants in Ankara, Turkey. *Social Forces* 51, 355–65.

Lewis, J. W., editor, 1971a: *The city in communist China*. Stanford: Stanford University Press. (449 pp.)

1971b: Commerce, education and political development in Tangshan, 1959–69. In Lewis, J. W., editor, 1971a, 153–82.

Lewis, O. 1959: *Five Families.* New York: Basic Books. (317 pp.)
  1966: The culture of poverty. *Scientific American* 215, 19–25.
Linsky, A. S. 1965: Some generalizations concerning primate cities. *Annals of the Association of American Geographers* 55, 506–13.
Lipman, A. 1969: *The Colombian entrepreneur in Bogota.* Coral Gables, Fla.: University of Miami Press. (144 pp.)
Lipset, S. M. and **Solari, A.**, editors, 1967: *Elites in Latin America.* New York: Oxford University Press. (529 pp.)
Little, K. 1965: *West African urbanization: a study of voluntary associations in social change.* London: Cambridge University Press. (179 pp.)
Lloyd, P. C. 1966: *The new elites of tropical Africa.* London: Oxford University Press. (390 pp.)
Lloyd, P. C., Mabogunje, A. L., and **Awe, B.,** editors, 1967: *The city of Ibadan.* New York: Cambridge University Press. (280 pp.)
Logan, M. I. 1972: The spatial system and planning strategies in developing countries. *Geographical Review* 62, 229–44.
Luttrell, W. 1972–3: Location planning and regional development in Tanzania. *Development and Change* IV, 17–38.
Lynch, O. 1968: The politics of untouchability: a case from Agra, India. In Singer, M. and Cohen, B., editors, 1968, 209–40.
Mabogunje, A. L. 1968: *Urbanization in Nigeria.* London: University of London Press. (353 pp.)
  1971: *Growth poles and growth centres in the regional development of Nigeria.* Geneva: United Nations Institute for Social Research. (81 pp.)
  1972: *Regional mobility and resource development in west Africa.* Montreal: McGill-Queen's University Press. (154 pp.)
  1973: Manufacturing and the geography of development in tropical Africa. *Economic Geography* 49, 1–19.
Maddick, H. 1963: *Democracy, decentralization and development.* Bombay: Asia Publishing House. (305 pp.)
Mamalakis, M. J. 1969: The theory of sectoral clashes. *Latin American Research Review* 4, 9–46.
Mangin, W. 1967: Latin American squatter settlements: a problem and a solution. *Latin American Research Review* 2, 65–98.
  1968: Poverty and politics in cities of Latin America. In Bloomberg, W., Jr. and Schmandt, H. J., editors, 1968, 397–432.
  editor, 1970: *Peasants in cities: readings in the anthropology of urbanization.* Boston: Houghton Mifflin. (207 pp.)
Marcus, J. 1973: Territorial organization of the lowland classic Maya. *Science* 180, 911–16.
Marris, P. 1961: *Family and social change in an African city.* London: Routledge and Kegan Paul. (179 pp.)
Marris, P. and **Somerset, A.** 1972: *The African entrepreneur: a study of*

entrepreneurship and development in Kenya. New York: Africana Publishing Corp. (288 pp.)

Marsden, K. 1971: Progressive technologies for developing countries. In Galenson, W., editor, 1971, 113–40.

    1974: The role of small-scale industry in development: opportunities and constraints. In Friedmann, J., editor, 1974b, 55–92.

Mayer, P. 1961: *Townsmen or tribesmen*. Cape Town: Oxford University Press. (329 pp.)

McElrath, D. 1965: Urban differentiation: problems and prospects. *Law and Contemporary Problems* 30, 103–10.

    1968: Societal scale and social differentiation: Accra, Ghana. In Greer, S., McElrath, D., Minar, D. and Orleans, P., 1968, 33–52.

McGee, T. G. 1967: *The Southeast Asian city*. London: Bell. (204 pp.)

    1971a: *The urbanization process in the Third World: explorations in search of a theory*. London: Bell. (179 pp.)

    1971b: Têtes de ponts et enclaves. Le probleme urbain et le processus d'urbanisation dans l'Asie du Sud-Est depuis 1945. *Revue Tiers-Monde* 12, 115–44.

    1973: Peasants in cities: a paradox, a paradox, a most ingenious paradox. *Human Organization* 32, 135–42.

    1974a: *Hawkers in Hong Kong. A study of policy and planning in a Third World city*. Centre of Asian Studies, Monograph Series, Hong Kong University.

    1974b: *The persistence of the proto-proletariat: occupational structures and planning for the future of Third World cities*. Comparative Urbanization Studies, School of Architecture and Urban Planning, University of California, Los Angeles. (70 pp.)

Meadows, P. and **Mizruchi, E. H.,** editors, 1969: *Urbanism, urbanization, and change: comparative perspectives*. Reading, Mass.: Addison-Wesley. (579 pp.)

Mehta, S. K. 1964: Some demographic and economic correlates of primate cities: a case for re-evaluation. *Demography* 1, 136–47.

Meillassoux, C. 1968: *Urbanization of an African community: voluntary associations in Bamako*. Seattle: University of Washington Press. (165 pp.)

Mellor, J. W. 1973: Accelerated growth in agricultural production and the intersectoral transfer of resources. *Economic Development and Cultural Change* 22, 1–16.

Mera, K. 1973: On the urban agglomeration and economic efficiency. *Economic Development and Cultural Change* 22, 309–24.

Merkx, G. W. 1969: Sectoral clashes and political change: the Argentine experience. *Latin American Research Review* 4, 89–116.

Mesa-Lago, C. 1972: *The labor force, employment, unemployment and under-*

employment in Cuba: 1899–1970. A Sage Professional Paper, International Studies Series 1. Beverley Hills: Sage. (71 pp.)

Metwally, M. M. and **Jensen, R. C.** 1973: A note on the measurement of regional income dispersion. *Economic Development and Cultural Change* 22, 135–6.

Miller, J. 1971a: Channelling national urban growth in Latin America. In Miller, J. and Gakenheimer, R., editors, 1971, 107–66.

1971b: The distribution of political and government power in the context of urbanization. In Miller, J. and Gakenheimer, R., editors, 1971, 211–34.

Miller, J. and **Gakenheimer, R.,** editors, 1971: *Latin American urban policies and the social sciences*. Beverley Hills: Sage. (398 pp.)

Miner, H. 1953: *The primitive city of Timbuctoo*. Princeton: Princeton University Press. (297 pp.)

editor, 1967: *The city in modern Africa*. London: Pall Mall Press. (354 pp.)

Mitchell, J. C., editor, 1969: *Social networks in urban situations*. Manchester: Manchester University Press. (378 pp.)

1970: Africans in industrial towns in Northern Rhodesia. In Mangin, W., editor, 1970, 160–70.

Mookherjee, D. and **Morrill, R. L.** 1973: *Urbanization in a developing economy: Indian perspectives and patterns*. A Sage Professional Paper, International Studies Series 2. Beverley Hills: Sage. (74 pp.)

Morris, F. B. and **Pyle, G. F.** 1971: The social environment of Rio de Janeiro in 1960. In Berry, B. J. L., editor, 1971a, 286–99.

Morse, R. M. 1958: *From community to metropolis: a biography of São Paulo, Brazil*. Gainesville, Fla.: University of Florida Press. (341 pp.)

1962: Latin American cities: aspects of function and structure. *Comparative Studies in Society and History* 4, 473–93.

1970a: *The limits of metropolitan dominance in contemporary Latin America*. Paper for the XXXIX Congress of Americanists, Lima, Peru. (16 pp.)

1970b: *International migrants and the urban ethos in Latin America*. Paper for the 7th World Congress of Sociology, Varna, Bulgaria. (40 pp.)

1971a: Planning, history, and politics: reflections on John Friedmann's 'The role of cities in national development'. In Miller, J. and Gakenheimer, R., editors, 1971, 189–200.

editor, 1971b: *The urban development of Latin America, 1750–1920*. Stanford: Stanford University, Center for Latin American Studies. (129 pp.)

1972: A prolegomenon to Latin American urban history. *The Hispanic American Historical Review* 52, 359–94.

Muller, H. J. 1952: *The uses of the past*. New York: Mentor. (384 pp.)

Mumford, L. 1961: *The city in history.* New York: Harcourt, Brace and World. (657 pp.)

Muñoz, H. and **de Olivera, O.** 1973: Migración interna y movilidad occupacional en la Ciudad de México. In Consejo Latinoamericano de Ciencias Sociales, *Migración y Desarrollo* 2, 83–98.

Nader, L. 1965: Communication between village and city in the modern Middle East. *Human Organization* 24, 18–24.

National Academy of Sciences, 1971: *Rapid population growth: consequences and policy implications,* Vol. 1. Baltimore: Johns Hopkins University Press.

Nelson, J. M. 1969: *Migrants, urban poverty, and instability in developing countries.* Occasional Papers in International Affairs 22, Harvard University, Center for International Affairs. (81 pp.)

Neutze, G. M. 1965: *Economic policy and the size of cities.* Canberra: The Australian National University. (136 pp.)

Nettl, J. P. 1967: *Political mobilization: a sociological analysis of methods and concepts.* New York: Basic Books. (442 pp.)

Nicholls, W. H. 1969: The transformation of agriculture in a semi-industrialized country: the case of Brazil. In Thornbecke, E., editor, 1969, 311–78.

Nie, N. H., Powell, G. B., Jr., and **Prewitt, K.** 1969: Social structure and political participation: developmental relations. *The American Political Science Review* 63, part I, 361–78; part II, 808–32.

Nun, J. 1969: Superpoblación relativa, ejercito industrial de reserva y masa marginal. *Revista Latinoamericana de Sociología* 5, 178–236.

O'Barr, W., Spain, D. and **Tessler, M.,** editors, 1973: *Survey research in Africa.* Evanston: Northwestern University Press. (349 pp.)

ODEPLAN, 1973: Tesis central de desarrollo espacial. *Revista Latinamericana de Estudios Urbano Regionales* 3, 147–60.

Orellana, C. L. 1973: Mixtec migrants in Mexico City: a case study of urbanization. *Human Organization* 32, 273–83.

Ottenberg, S. 1962: The development of local government in a Nigerian township. *Anthropologica* 4, 121–61.

Owen, C. and **Witton, R. A.** 1973: National division and mobilization: a reinterpretation of primacy. *Economic Development and Cultural Change* 21, 325–37.

Owusu, M. 1970: *Uses and abuses of political power: a case study of continuity and change in the politics of Ghana.* Chicago: University of Chicago Press.

Parkin, D. 1969: *Neighbors and nationals in an African city ward.* Berkeley: University of California Press. (228 pp.)

Peattie, L. R. 1968: *The view from the barrio.* Ann Arbor: University of Michigan Press. (147 pp.)

Pedersen, P. O. 1970: Innovation diffusion within and between national urban systems. *Geographical Analysis* 2, 203–54.

Peil, M. 1972: The Ghanaian factory worker: industrial man in Africa. *African Studies Series* 5. New York: Cambridge University Press. (254 pp.)

Perlman, J. 1971: *The fate of migrants in Rio's favelas.* MIT: Unpublished Ph.D. dissertation.

Perloff, H. S., editor, 1969: *The quality of the urban environment.* Baltimore: The Johns Hopkins University Press. (332 pp.)

Petersen, K. K. 1971: Villagers in Cairo: hypotheses versus data. *American Journal of Sociology* 77, 560–73.

Pitts, F. R. 1971: Factorial ecology of Seoul and Taegu, Korea: a preliminary report. In Berry, B. J. L., editor, 1971a, 300–2.

Plotnicov, L. 1967: *Strangers to the city: urban man in Jos, Nigeria.* Pittsburgh: University of Pittsburgh Press. (320 pp.)

1970: The modern African elite of Jos, Nigeria. In Tuden, A. and Plotnicov, L., editors, 1970, 269–302.

Polanyi, K., Arsenberg, C. M., and **Pearson, H. W.,** editors, 1957: *Trade and market in the early empires.* Glencoe, Ill.: Free Press and Falcon's Wing Press. (382 pp.)

Pons, V. 1969: *Stanleyville.* London: Oxford University Press. (356 pp.)

Portes, A. 1970: El proceso de urbanización y su impacto en la modernizacion de las instituciones políticas locales. *Revista SIAP* 4, 5–21.

1972: Rationality in the slum: an essay in interpretive sociology. *Comparative Studies in Society and History* 14, 268–86.

Powell, S. 1969: Political participation in the Barriadas: a case study. *Comparative Political Studies* 2, 195–215.

Prakash, V. 1969: *New towns in India.* Monograph 8, Program in Comparative Studies on Southern Asia, Duke University. Detroit: Cellar Book Shops. (149 pp.)

Pred, A. R. 1973a: The growth and development of systems of cities in advanced economies. In Pred, A. R. and Tornqvist, G. E., 1973, *Systems of cities and information flows.* Lund Studies in Geography, Ser. B, Human Geography 38. Lund: C. W. K. Gleerup, 9–82.

1973b: *Urban growth and the circulation of information: the United States system of cities, 1790–1840.* Cambridge, Mass.: Harvard University Press. (348 pp.)

Rabinovitz, F. F. 1969: Urban development and political development in Latin America. In Daland, R. T., editor, 1969, 88–123.

1973: The study of urban politics and the politics of urban studies. In Wulff, R., editor, 1973b, 83–100.

Rabinovitz, F. and **Trueblood, F.** 1971: *Latin American urban research,* Beverley Hills: Sage Publications.

Rabushka, A. 1971: Integration in urban Malaysia: ethnic attitudes among Malayans and Chinese. *Journal of Asian and African Studies* 6, 91–107.

Ratinoff, L. 1967: The new urban groups: the middle classes. In Lipset, S. M. and Solari, A., editors, 1967, 61–93.

Ray, T. 1969: *The politics of the barrios of Venezuela*. Berkeley: University of California Press. (211 pp.)

Redfield, R. 1953: *The primitive world and its transformations*. Ithaca: Cornell University Press. (185 pp.)

Redfield, R. and **Singer, M.** 1954: The cultural role of cities. *Economic Development and Cultural Change* 3, 53–73.

Reina, R. E. 1973: *Parand: social boundaries in an Argentine city*. Austin: University of Texas Press. (390 pp.)

Reissman, L. 1964: *The urban process: cities in industrial society*. New York: The Free Press of Glencoe. (255 pp.)

Reyna, J. L. 1972: Occupational mobility: the Mexican case. In Davis, S. M., and Goodman, J. W., editors, 1972, 111–18.

Richardson, H. W. 1973: *The economics of urban size*. Lexington, Mass.: Saxon House/Lexington Books. (243 pp.)

Richardson, I. L. 1973: *Urban government for Rio de Janeiro*. New York: Praeger.

Riddell, J. B. 1970: *The spatial dynamics of modernization in Sierra Leone: structure, diffusion, and response*. Evanston: Northwestern University Press. (142 pp.)

Riddell, J. B. and **Harvey, M.** 1972: The urban system in the migration process: an evaluation of step-wise migration in Sierra Leone. *Economic Geography* 48, 270–83.

Ridker, R. R. 1971: Employment and unemployment in Near East and South Asian countries: a review of evidence and issues. In Ridker and Lubell, 1971, 6–58.

Ridker, R. R. and **Lubell, H.,** editors, 1971: *Employment and unemployment of the Near East and South Asia*. Vol. I. Delhi: Vikas Publications. (470 pp.)

Riggs, F. W. 1964: *Administration in developing countries: the theory of prismatic society*. Boston: Houghton Mifflin. (477 pp.)

Rivière d'Arc, H. 1973: *Guadalajara y su region*. Mexico City: SepSetentas. (228 pp.)

Rivkin, M. D. 1965: *Area development for national growth: the Turkish precedent*. New York: Praeger. (228 pp.)

Roberts, B. 1968: Politics in a neighbourhood of Guatemala. *Sociology* (London) 2, 185–204.

1970: *Migration and population growth in Guatemala City: implications for social and economic development*. Centre for Latin American Studies, Monograph Series 2, University of Liverpool. (35 pp.)

1972: *Organizing strangers: poor families in Guatemala City.* Austin: University of Texas Press. (300 pp.)

Robson, W. A. and **Regan, D. E.,** editors, 1972: *Great cities of the world: their government, politics, and planning.* London: Allen and Unwin. (814 pp.)

Rodwin, L. 1963: Choosing regions for development. In Friedrich, C. J. and Harris, S. E., editors, *Public Policy.* A yearbook of the Harvard University Graduate School of Public Administration, Vol. 12, Cambridge, Mass.: Harvard University Press, 141–62.

1970: *Nations and cities: a comparison of strategies for urban growth.* Boston: Houghton Mifflin. (395 pp.)

Rodwin, L. and **Associates** 1969: *Planning urban growth and regional development: the experience of the Guayana program in Venezuela.* Cambridge, Mass.: The MIT Press. (524 pp.)

Rofman, A. B. 1972: El fenómeno de la concentración y centralización espacial en America Latina: elementos para una discusión. *Revista Latinoamericana de Estudios Urbano Regionales* 3, 11–34.

Rofman, A. B. and **Romero, L. A.** 1973: *Sistema socioeconómico y estructura regional en la Argentina.* Buenos Aires: Amorrotu. (227 pp.)

Rogler, L. H. 1967: Slum neighborhoods in Latin America. *Journal of Inter-american Studies* 9, 507–28.

Rollwagen, J. 1972: A comparative framework for the investigation of city-as-context: a discussion of the Mexican case. *Urban Anthropology* 1, 68–87.

Rosenthal, D. B. 1970: *The limited elite: politics and government in two Indian cities.* Chicago: University of Chicago Press. (360 pp.)

Ross, M. H. 1972: *The political integration of urban squatters.* Evanston: Northwestern University Press.

Rosser, C. 1972a: Housing and planned urban change: the Calcutta experience. In Dwyer, D. J., editor, 1972, 179–90.

1972b: *Urbanization in tropical Africa: a demographic introduction.* The Ford Foundation, International Urbanization Survey. (74 pp.)

Rowe, W. L. 1973: Caste, kinship and association in urban India. In Southall, A., editor, 1973, 211–50.

Rozman, G. 1973: *Urban networks in Ch'ing China and Tokugawa Japan.* Princeton: Princeton University Press.

Ruttan, V. W. 1974: Rural development programs: a skeptical perspective. In Friedmann, J., editor, 1974b, 5–44.

Safier, M., editor, 1970: *The role of urban and regional planning in national development of East Africa.* Kampala: Milton Obote Foundation. (299 pp.)

Salter, C. L. 1974: Chinese experiments in urban space: the quest for an agropolitan China. In Friedmann, J., editor, 1974b, 101–26.

87

Santos, M. 1971: *Les villes du tiers monde*. Paris: M-Th. Genin. (428 pp.)

Schmidt, C. F. 1973: *The South African regional system: political independence in an interacting space economy*. Faculty of Science, University of South Africa: Unpublished Ph.D. dissertation. (317 pp.)

Schnore, L. F. 1965: On the spatial structure of cities in the two Americas. In Hauser, P. M. and Schnore, L. F., editors, 1965, 347–98.

Schnore, L. F. and **Fagin, H.**, editors, 1967: *Urban research and policy planning*. Beverley Hills: Sage. (638 pp.)

Schteingart, M., editor, 1973: *Urbanización y dependencia en América Latina*. Bueno Aires: SIAP. (372 pp.)

Schumpeter, J. A. 1951: *The theory of economic development*. Cambridge, Mass.: Harvard University Press. (255 pp.)

Schwab, W. B. 1970: Urbanism, corporate groups and culture change in Africa. *Anthropological Quarterly* 43, 187–214.

Schwirian, K. P. and **Smith, R. K.** 1969: *Primacy, modernization, and urban structure: the ecology of Puerto Rican cities*. Working Paper in Human Ecology 5, Ohio State University.

Sendut, H. 1965: The structure of Kuala Lumpur, Malaysia's capital city. *Town Planning Review* 35, 125–38.

1966: City size distribution in Southeast Asia. *Journal of Asian Studies* 4, 268–80.

Shachar, A. 1971: Israel's development towns: evaluation of national urbanization policy. *Journal of the American Institute of Planners*, 362–72.

Shack, W. A. 1973: Urban ethnicity and cultural process of urbanization in Ethiopia. In Southall, A., editor, 1973, 251–86.

Shah, A. M. 1973: *The household dimension of the family in India*. Berkeley: University of California Press.

Shah, S. M. 1974: Growth centers as a strategy for rural development: India experience. *Economic Development and Cultural Change* 22, 215–28.

Sherwood, F. P. 1967: *Institutionalizing the grass roots in Brazil: a study in comparative local government*. San Francisco: Chandler. (173 pp.)

Singer, M. 1972: *When a great tradition modernizes*. New York: Praeger. (430 pp.)

Singer, M. and **Cohen, B.**, editors, 1968: *Structure and change in Indian society*. Viking Fund Publications in Anthropology 47. (507 pp.)

Skinner, G. W. 1968: *The city in Chinese society*. Unpublished paper. (25 pp.)

Smith, R. H. T. and **Hay, A. M.** 1970: *Interregional trade and money flows in Nigeria, 1964*. Ibadan: Oxford University Press. (254 pp.)

Smith, R. J. 1973: Town and city in pre-modern Japan: small families, small households, and residential instability. In Southall, A., editor, 1973, 163–210.

Smith, T. C., editor, 1960: *City and village in Japan: economic development and cultural change*. Chicago: University of Chicago Press. (257 pp.)

Smythe, H. H. and **Smythe, M. M.** 1960: *The new Nigerian elite*. Stanford: Stanford University Press. (196 pp.)

Soja, E. W. 1968: *The geography of modernization in Kenya: a spatial analysis of social, economic, and political change*. Syracuse: Syracuse University Press. (143 pp.)

1969: A paradigm for the geographical analysis of political systems. In Cox, K., Reynolds, D., and Rokkan, S., editors, 1974.

1973: Comparative urbanization studies. In Wulff, R., editor, 1973b, 1–19.

Soja, E. W. and **Tobin, R. J.** (in press): The geography of modernization: paths, patterns, and processes of spatial change in developing countries. In Brunner, R. and Brewer, G., editors (in press).

Southall, A., editor, 1973: *Urban anthropology*. New York: Oxford University Press. (489 pp.)

Sovani, N. V. 1964: The analysis of 'overurbanization'. *Economic Development and Cultural Change* 12, 113–22.

Spengler, J. J. 1967: Africa and the theory of optimum city size. In Miner, H., editor, 1967, 55–90.

Spengler, O. 1926–28: *The decline of the West: perspectives of world history*. 2 vols. New York: Knopf. (428 and 507 pp.)

Spodek, H. 1973: Urban politics in the local kingdoms of India: a view for the princely capitals of Saurashtra under British rule. *Modern Asian Studies* 7, 253–75.

Stallings, B. 1972: *Economic dependency in Africa and Latin America*. A Sage Professional Paper, Comparative Politics Series 3. Beverley Hills: Sage. (60 pp.)

Stanford Research Institute 1969: *Costs of urban infrastructure for industry as related to its size in developing countries: India case study*. Menlo Park CA: Stanford Research Institute. (435 pp.)

Stea, D. and **Wood, D.** (forthcoming): *A cognitive atlas: the psychological geography of four Mexican cities*.

Stephenson, G. V. 1970: Two newly created capitals: Islamabad and Brasilia. *Town Planning Review* 41, 317–32.

Stöhr, W. B. 1972: *El desarrollo regional en América Latina: experiencias y perspectivas*. Buenos Aires: Ed. SIAP. (244 pp.)

Stren, R. 1972: Urban policy in Africa: a political analysis. *African Studies Review* 15, 489–516.

Stuckey, B., editor, 1973–4: Espaces Africaines: dépendence ou développement? *Espaces et Sociétés* (Special Number) 10 and 11.

Sunkel, O. No date: 'Transactional capitalism and nation disintegration in Latin America.' Unpublished paper.

Szyliowicz, J. S. 1966: *Erdemli: political change in rural Turkey.* The Hague: Mouton. (218 pp.)

Tanabe, K. 1959: The development of spatial structure in Japanese cities with regard to castle towns. *Science Reports of Tôhoku University.* Seventh Series, Geography 8, 88–105.

1970: Intra-regional structure of Japanese cities. In *Annals of The Association of Japanese Geographers,* 1970, 109–20.

Tangri, S. 1962: Urbanization, political stability, and economic growth. In Turner, R., editor, 1962, 192–212.

Taylor, G. 1946: *Our evolving civilization: an introduction of geopacifics.* Toronto: University of Toronto Press. (370 pp.)

Tekeli, I. 1973: Evolution of spatial organization in the Ottoman Empire and Turkish Republic. In Brown, L. C., editor, 1973, 244–76.

The Industrial Research Unit, Department of Economics, University of Ife 1972: *Small-scale industries—western state Nigeria.* Ide-Ife, Nigeria.

Thodey, A. R. 1969: *Analysis of staple food price behavior in western Nigeria.* Department of Agricultural Economics, University of Illinois, Urbana, Ill.: Ph.D. dissertation.

Thornbecke, E., editor, 1969: *The role of agriculture in economic development.* New York: Columbia University Press.

Timms, D. W. G. 1971: *The urban mosaic.* Cambridge: Cambridge University Press. (277 pp.)

Todaro, M. 1971: Income expectations, rural–urban migration, and employment in Africa. *International Labor Review,* 387–413.

Tuden, A. and **Plotnicov, L.** 1970; Social stratification in Africa. New York: Free Press. (349 pp.)

Turner, J. F. C. 1968a: Uncontrolled urban settlements: problems and policies. *International Social Development Review* 1, New York: United Nations, 107–28.

1968b: Housing priorities, settlement patterns, and urban development in modernizing countries. *Journal of the American Institute of Planners* 34, 354–63.

Turner, J. F. C. and **Fichter, R.,** editors, 1972: *Freedom to build.* New York: Macmillan. (301 pp.)

Turner, R. 1941: *The great cultural traditions.* 2 vols. New York: McGraw-Hill. (1333 pp.)

Turner, R., editor, 1962: *India's urban future.* Berkeley: University of California Press. (470 pp.)

Turnham, D. and **Jaeger, I.** 1971: *The employment problem in less developed countries: a review of the evidence.* Paris: OECD: (154 pp.)

Ucko, P. J., Tringham, R. and **Dimbleby, G. W.,** editors, 1972: *Man, settlement and urbanism.* Cambridge, Mass.: Schenkman. (979 pp.)

United Nations, 1968: World urbanization trends, 1920–1960. *International Social Development Review* 1, 9–20.

1969: *Growth of the world's urban and rural population, 1920–2000.* New York: Department of Social Affairs. (124 pp.)

1971: *1970 Report on the world social situation.* New York: Department of Social Affairs. (231 pp.)

United Nations Regional Planning Mission to Thailand, 1968: *A preliminary survey of the northern region of Thailand.* Draft report. (Mimeo.)

Uzzell, D. 1974: A strategic analysis of social structure in Lima, Peru, using the concept of 'plays.' *Urban Anthropology* 3, 34–46.

van Raay, H. G. T. 1970–71: A case for regional planning and a statement of intent. *Development and Change* 2, 1–21.

Vapnarsky, C. A. 1969: On rank-size distribution of cities: an ecological approach. *Economic Development and Cultural Change* 17, 584–95.

Vatuk, S. 1973: *Kinship and urbanization: white collar migrants in north India.* Berkeley: University of California Press. (219 pp.)

Viloria, L. A. 1972: The Manileños: significant elites in urban development and nation-building in the Philippines. In Dwyer, D. J., editor, 1972, 16–28.

Vincent, J. 1971: *African elite: the big men of a small town.* New York and London: Columbia University Press. (309 pp.)

Walsh, A. H. 1968: *The urban challenge to government: an international comparison of thirteen cities.* New York: Praeger. (294 pp.)

1969: Urban local government in French-speaking Africa. *Africa Urban Notes* 4, 1–34.

Ward, R. E. 1960: Urban–rural differences and the process of political modernization in Japan: a case study. In Smith, T. C., editor, 1960, 135–66.

Weaver, T. and **White, D.,** editors, 1972: *The anthropology of urban environments.* Boulder, Colorado: The Society for Applied Anthropology. (136 pp.)

Weber, A. F. 1965: *The growth of cities in the nineteenth century: a study in statistics.* Ithaca: Cornell University Press. (495 pp.)

Weber, M. 1958: *The city.* Glencoe, Ill.: Free Press. (242 pp.)

Weiner, M. 1967: Urbanization and political protest. *Civilizations* 17, 44–52.

1971: Political demography: an inquiry into the political consequences of population change. In National Academy of Sciences, 1971, 507–617.

Weisner, T. 1973: Studying rural–urban ties: a matched network sample from Kenya. In O'Barr, W., Spain, D. and Tessler, M., 1973, 122–34.

Werlin, H. H. 1966: The Nairobi city council: a study in comparative local government. *Comparative Studies in Society and History* 8, 181–98.

Wheatley, P. 1963: What the greatness of the city is said to be—reflection on Sjoberg. *Pacific Viewpoint* 4, 163–88.

1971: *The pivot of the four quarters: preliminary enquiry into the origins and character of the ancient Chinese city.* Chicago: Aldine. (602 pp.)

Whitten, N. E. 1965: *Class, kinship and power in an Ecuadorian town.* Stanford: Stanford University Press. (238 pp.)

Whitten, N. E. and **Wolfe, A. W.** 1973: Network analysis. In Honigmann, J. J., editor, 1973, 717–46.

Wilkie, R. W. 1968: *On the theory of process in human geography: a case study of migration in rural Argentina.* Department of Geography, University of Washington: Unpublished Ph.D. dissertation.

Wilkinson, T. O. 1965: *The urbanization of Japanese labor, 1868–1955.* Amherst, Mass.: The University of Massachusetts Press. (243 pp.)

Williams, B. A. and **Walsh, A. H.** 1968: *Urban government for metropolitan Lagos.* New York: Praeger. (182 pp.)

Williamson, J. G. 1965: Regional inequality and the process of national development: a description of the patterns. *Economic Development and Cultural Change* 13, 3–45.

Willig, R. 1973: Estructura y transformación de la planificación urbana y regional dependiente. *Revista Latinoamericana de Estudios Urbano Regionales* 3, 175–86.

Wilson, M. and **Mafeje, A.** 1963: *Langa: a study of social groupings in an African township.* London University Press. (190 pp.)

Wingo, L., Jr. 1967: Recent patterns of urbanization among Latin American countries. *Urban Affairs Quarterly* 2, 81–109.

Wittfogel, K. A. 1957: *Oriental despotism: A comparative study of total power.* New Haven: Yale University Press. (553 pp.)

Wolpe, H. 1974: *Urban politics in Nigeria: a study of Port Harcourt.* Berkeley: University of California Press.

World Bank 1972: *Urbanization: sector working paper.* Baltimore: Johns Hopkins Press. (111 pp.)

Wu, Y. L. 1967: *The spatial economy of communist China: a study of industrial location and transportation.* New York: Praeger. (367 pp.)

Wulff, R. 1973a: Resources in the comparative study of urbanization. School of Architecture and Urban Planning, University of California, Los Angeles, *Comparative Urbanization Studies.* (50 pp.)

editor, 1973b: Research traditions in the comparative study of urbanization. *Comparative Urbanization Studies.* School of Architecture and Urban Planning, University of California, Los Angeles. (150 pp.)

Yazai-k T. 1968: *Social change in the city in Japan: from earliest times through the industrial revolution.* San Francisco: Japan Publications Trading Co. (589 pp.)

Zachariah, K. C. 1969: Bombay migration study: a pilot analysis of migration to an Asian metropolis. In Breese, G., editor, 1969, 360–75.

Index